Catching up on the news.

Coasting Bargemaster

Coasting Bargemaster

BY

Bob Roberts

ILLUSTRATED

SEAFARER BOOKS
2000

First published 1949
St. Anne's Press Timperley

This edition published in 2000 in the UK by
Seafarer Books
102 Redwald Road, Rendlesham,
Woodbridge,
Suffolk, IP12 2TE

UK ISBN 0-9538180-1-2

Typesetting by Julie Rainford
Cover design by Louis Mackay

Cover shows Bob Roberts at wheel of *Martinet* with
barge *Martinet* in background

Printed in Finland by WS Bookwell, Juva

Contents

For all the working
barges and the men who
sailed them.

Foreword

The Thames Estuary sea-scape is one of horizontals: bars of dun green, grey, ochre, distant ragged breakers, cloud-shadow and the white dazzle of wet sand. Once, the only vertical objects were the leaning brown towers of the sailing barges.

This was Bob Robert's world of sandbank and swatchway where life was lived to a stop-go rhythm of fair tide and foul, head wind and fair. Anchoring until the stream favoured, then mustering and striding up-river on a young flood with the shores reeling by. Nowadays the pressing of a starter button solves most of the sailor's problems; this book tells how it was. Anybody who sails can but be the richer for reading it.

To my sorrow I only sailed with Bob in *Cambria* three or four times but on each occasion I came away tipsy on barge-lore, proselytising on the art of seamanship and feeling that I was returning from the past. Carrying a cargo set you apart from mere yachtsmen, carrying it under sail set you apart from the world. Bob altered my concept of sailing and gave me my deep love of the old ways.

He was a bargemaster in all that the title implies. He could luff and shoot a lock gate, carrying his way clean across a basin to his berth. 'Depends on your cargo, cement's heavy, cattle-feed's lighter.' He knew the banks and swatchways, where he could bang a leeboard and cheat, where he could anchor and wait a tide to lie ringed by sands as the tide ebbed. His ancient skills shine out of these pages.

I remember his lurching gait and huge, battered hands, his vast tooth-gappy grin. Everywhere he went people hailed him and grinned. 'Give us a song Bob,' and he would roll up his sleeves, stick a boot up on a chair, grin that grin and strike a chord on his squeeze-box.

Pomposity was anathema to him and inspired him to shock. Once, he was faced by a stuffed-shirt audience, 'Left me teeth back aboard the barge' he proclaimed, 'and I've got a boil on me arse but I'll do me best!' This book is about barges, sailormen, barge owners and the hard old days. He once told me of times when a skipper and mate might go to sea with half a loaf of bread between them, leaving their grub ashore for missus and kids. A fast passage meant profit, and a slow one hunger.

He possessed a poet's sensitivity. He told me of an old skipper ruminating on hard times when a heading wind could mean hunger. …'Then it'd come ahead and we'd have to wind (tack) 'er and that old stay'sl sheet would rattle and go "Nothin-ter-come, nothin-ter-come, nothin-ter-come…! A stark poetry.

Bob is around no longer but his grin is immortal, like that Cheshire cat which faded from view – all save for its great, glorious, gappy grin.

Des Sleightholme, Hope Cove.

Preface

SAILORS WHO HAVE BEEN BRED to their trade beneath a spread of canvas, with nothing but the wind and tide and their own good foresight to bring them safely home, are becoming few and hard to find.

Here and there, in the corner of some waterside tavern, or pottering about on a small shipyard, you will find occasionally some hoary-headed old stalwart who will spin you a tale (if you have time and patience to listen) of his days in square-rigged ships. But the last of such as he are now close to the grave and the only men of their kind, who know how much a shift of wind, another hour's tide or perhaps a deathly calm can mean to the safety of a ship, her cargo and the lives of her crew, are the men and lads who man the wind-driven vessels which ply in coastal waters.

These coastal vessels used to be the training ground for many of our most famous deep-sea sailormen. The sharp wits and watchfulness required to handle a ship under sail in narrow tidal waters, with the nearness of land more of a danger than a comfort in heavy gales, bring out all the qualities required to make a really first-class seaman. The great Captain Cook learnt the art of sailing in an East Coast collier, and even the gallant Sir Francis Drake had the rudiments of the sea dinned into him aboard a Kentish Hoy, a small, shallow-draft type of barge frequently to be seen in the waters of the Thames Estuary in his days.

With the passing of the square-rig men, the coastal sailing barges, schooners and ketches maintained for a time a rich source of sail-trained men. In turn, the sturdy wooden and steel schooners which used to be seen in large numbers on the West Coast and in the Channel have had their day, and their skippers and mates who are not retired, too old, or dead, have passed into the easier life of power-driven ships.

Surviving all these splendid men and ships is the fleet of coastal sailing barges which trade from London to the East Coast ports and sometimes down-Channel. Their numbers are dwindling but their red-dressed canvas is still a feature of London River. The boom-rigged barges have all gone (the last of them holds a prominent place in this book) but the spritsailed ones are still holding their own in the Estuary trade and beyond.

Here, then, we find the last of the sailormen. Soon they, too, may be swept away by the mechanical monstrosities that have usurped the title of 'ships'.

Before sailing barges and sailing bargemen have faded into a forgotten age, I set myself to write this story of some of my own experiences as a coasting sailor. I have boldly started with the last of my days in the schooners, but when I came to the years spent in sailing barges I found a good deal more to write about than I expected. I have skipped from year to year in a matter of a few lines. The time I spent on the East Coast in a big steel spritsail barge in the years of the Second World War and after I have not even touched upon, and this will have to be laid aside or perhaps one day form material for another book. In the meantime I trust that the reader will get from this volume a taste of salt water, a breath of good clean air and an insight into the life of the men who gain their livelihood by their knowledge of wind and tide.

A. W. R.

Illustrations

Chapter One

A SOUTH-WEST GALE and a heavy sea off the southern coast of Ireland, a sixty-year-old schooner, short-handed and with a gushing leak, bring to a mariner's mind all the portents of wreck and disaster.

That was the situation the mate and I had to face one winter's night many years ago. I thought the schooner was going to sink and I believe the mate did too, although he did not venture an opinion. It was moonlight and I could just see his massive form working doggedly at one of the midship pumps. We both held shares in the vessel and were desperate to save her; but the nearest land was twenty-five miles away and a dead lee shore, open to the full fury of the Atlantic weather.

We were the only two on board—the mate and I—for the reason that the last of our crew had left us in Wexford and we had sailed the day after, which was Christmas Day. And to try and find a seaman to ship away to sea at such a festive time, especially in Ireland, is to set oneself on a hopeless search.

Bound for Falmouth, we had decided to take the risk of getting her round the Longships, crew or no crew. An easy enough task in ordinary weather, or even bad weather be the ship tight. But the poor old schooner, for all her teak planking and oak timbers, was spewing her caulking out and beating the pumps every hour.

Sometimes we took turns at pumping, other times leaving the wheel unattended to work a pump each—for there were two big patent ones forward of the mainmast.

Forty-eight hours we had had of this and already there was a good four feet of water sloshing to and fro in her hold, creeping up into the chart room and quarters aft, filling everywhere with a slime of the loam and gravel with which we were loaded.

She could not last forever like that, and likely as not would founder within the next twenty-four hours even if the weather moderated. There was one port dead to leeward of us—Waterford, with its entrance in the recess of a rock-strewn bay. I had never been there and on my general chart the place was marked about as big as a pinprick. There was the powerful Hook Light to guide us if we could but pick up the bay accurately, but one mistake and we should be thrown up among the surf on a rocky deathbed without a hope of saving either the ship or ourselves.

'Bout oh !' There was nothing left now but to let her run to leeward. As she came off the wind with the helm hard up, the foresail blew to pieces, rent from luff to leech and down along the head-rope as well.

I could not leave the wheel as the old vessel bore away, lest she broach-to, and the mate struggled with the flogging cracking ribbons of canvas alone as he let go the halliards. He was too tired to swear and curse as is the habit of schooner mates in such circumstances. He got the spars lashed together, muzzled the remnants with gaskets and without a word returned to the pumps.

'Blinking dark, ain't it,' was his only comment as we changed over. Whether he was referring to our prospects or the weather I do not know.

We sighted the Hook Light in the small hours of the morning. It was slightly on our port bow. With the wind tending to wester we could have got her round the Coningbeg lightship to Wexford Bay (a much safer refuge to make) had not the water in the hold made her almost unmanageable when the seas were abeam. We did get our mainsheet in to try her but it was no use. She just wallowed her covering board under when the water in her shot to leeward. So we squared away again for the Hook.

The Hook is a flat rocky promontory, and I knew from conversation with other skippers that there was a shallow ledge to the westward of it. Bucking, rolling and wallowing, the ship seemed to be approaching the shore at a tremendous pace. We could hear the thunder of surf and once when a giant curling crest swept under us I must confess my heart appeared to miss a couple of beats. But I have always found that a full realisation of danger makes one all the more determined in face of it.

We were close to the light, so close that by its flash we could see a mass of wildly careering surf. The mate left the pump and started to sound with the hand lead.

No bottom at seven. No bottom at ten, then six fathoms. Several casts more and he called five. I shifted my helm then and ran her into the bay.

Somewhere inside that bay the river Suir issued, and until we could get up the river there was no semblance of shelter. The noise of the wind and surf forced us to shout at the top of our voices to make each other hear and understand.

The schooner steered madly. As her stern lifted the water in her would run forward and force the ship against her helm. More than once I had to get the wheel over from hard up to hard down to keep her from slewing round beam on to the sea. And all the time she was rushing on to what seemed inevitable destruction. Our only chance was to sound our way round the eastern edge of the bay until we found the river entrance.

The mate armed the base of the lead with tallow so that with each cast he could get a sample of the nature of the bottom. But it only descended on hard sand and rock.

The sensation of standing at the wheel can only be likened to driving a mad horse at a precipice. I could see the lights of Dunmore to the westward and began to wonder if we had missed the river after all. If such was the case the ship was as good as a wreck and in the back of my mind I decided to make the ending

as near Dunmore as possible so that there might be a dog's
chance of saving ourselves.

'Three—soft bottom—mud.'

Those words, shouted raucously by a powerful man at the top
of his voice, sounded to me sweeter than anything I have ever
heard.

We were in.

Two leading lights showed up, then two more. The thunder of
surf faded away astern. The water became smooth and seemed
very quiet. A church clock ashore struck three. A dog barked.

'Let go.'

Splash, clang. The anchor went down and the chain rattled
cheerfully through the hawse pipe. We dropped the sails and sat
down on the main hatch.

It was all over.

· · · · ·

We signalled two hobblers at break of day and they helped us
beach the schooner on a sandy flat off the tiny village of Passage
East.

A little crowd assembled. Lloyd's agent arrived. A busybody
country customs official took it into his head to report to the
Board of Trade that we had come in 'in distress'. They sent an
official surveyor to specify what repairs were necessary.

She was an old ship and she had been badly strained. And the
surveyor was hard and uncompromising. Estimates for repairs
soared to preposterous levels. Even the local hobblers wanted a
ridiculous sum to help shift her to a mud bank further up the
river. Money—money—money, that's what they all wanted—
stretching out their hands like a lot of vultures to grab from us the
last of our meagre resources and the last drop of life-blood from
the old ship. It was a long time since she had paid her way and
there was no bag of sovereigns left to aid her now.

Yet she was not so badly damaged by the gale as I had
thought. With some spiking and caulking she could have been
made fit to resume her passage. We could get a new foresail sent
from Arklow. A shipwright was willing to do the repairs for
twenty-five pounds, but he was squeezed out by much higher and
grander estimates which the surveyor seemed more inclined to

approve of. From the original and reasonable twenty-five pounds the final tender reached over five hundred, and the surveyor suggested that if we spent that amount he would probably allow the schooner to resume trading.

I felt very bitter about it all. Those forty-eight hours on the pumps, that hair-raising run for a lee shore—all for this. We had nowhere near enough money to satisfy these vultures. We might just as well have let her smash up or signalled for a lifeboat to take us off and abandoned her at sea.

Had we been able to patch her up and the weather been half decent the mate and I would have sailed her to sea one night to hell knows where; just for the sake of thwarting those who sought to take advantage of our misfortunes. A friend wired me a hundred pounds, but I sent it back. What would a hundred pounds have been among these people?

· · · · ·

A few weeks later there was an auction sale a little way up-river from Passage East. The schooner was sold to the highest bidder. Into the hands of cheap-jacks and mean people went the mahogany furniture from the cabin, the old weather glass and ship's clock, and the little white plaster lady which had coyly nestled under the schooner's arrogant bowsprit.

It had to be. We were broke.

· · · · ·

So I left the sea, went back to England, and worked ashore, trying to convince myself that no one with any sense ever went to sea, especially in sail. The shore held great possibilities for a man, I argued with myself, opportunities to plan and prospects of rich reward for his labours; whereas the sea held out nothing but the prospect of years of hard work, long hours, sleepless nights and but little in the way of hard cash. And I believe that I would there and then have finished with going to sea and satisfied myself with a bit of yachting had I not been fool enough to take a job within easy access of the Port of London.

More and bigger ships were using the river, and once or twice

I spent my spare hours walking the banks of the lower reaches, watching the interminable stream of traffic on the tideway. Great liners stood out like giants among the myriads of tugs and lighters, the bustling colliers from the north, and crowds of small Dutch motor ships, which at that time were collaring our coastal trade with cheap freights. But it was the red-sailed sailing barges that took my fancy as they threaded their way to and fro, looking very stately and dignified amidst that horde of power driven, smoke-grimed, soulless ruffians. For all their slab sides and flat bottoms the barges were real ships in comparison with the noisy mechanical contraptions which were forever threatening to run them down.

The amazing sailing qualities of these barges and the skill of their crews had always been highly praised by schooner men who used to come to Erith with china clay from the Cornish ports. I remember old Charlie Deacon, the veteran skipper of the barquentine *Waterwitch* (in which ship I had been drilled in the elements of seamanship) telling me that 'You can't beat a bargeman in a tideway'. And old Charlie was reckoned pretty smart himself in close waters.

I was standing by the lock gates of the Royal Albert Dock one day and a grey steel barge named the *Reminder* was waiting to go out into the river. She lay in the lock with her topsail sheet out, looking rather gawky and awkward among the bunch of craft around her. Then as the lock gates opened there came a rattle of her topsail halliard block, the screech of a brail winch, a fluttering of white canvas as the big staysail went up the topmast stay; and within a matter of moments she was a cloud of sail. All this was done by two men, the skipper and mate, an impossible feat in any other type of vessel. These barges only carry two men except the very big ones who have three on long coastal voyages.

But it was the sight of the *Reminder* going out of the dock that day and sailing away in the sunshine down Gallions Reach towards her own peaceful Essex shore that finally put paid to my ideas of settling down ashore.

Before I quite realised what I was about or had considered the consequences of my actions, I found myself mate of the sailing barge *Audrey*, trimming coal at Beckton Gasworks where we were loading for Southend. And was I sorry? Well, that was a long time ago and I'm not sorry yet. For, although the schooners

were nearly all gone, here was a new life, a new world, but it was
still a world of sail. And the training I had had with gaffs and
booms and square-sail yards stood me in good stead in this new
and complicated spritsail rig. Before a year had passed I was out
of the river work and shipped as mate in several of the big
coasters which traded from London to the Humber and down
Channel. And in due course I became master.

So after all these years I have sat down to write this tale of
sailing barges, of slashing breezes and bellying red canvas, of a
world which perhaps you did not know even existed, so different
is it from the workaday life of the ordinary citizen. I will not
claim it as a pretty story of an idealistic life which will send the
romantic-minded seeking a berth in a sailing barge, because such
a romanticist would only end up a disillusioned and embittered
fool. But it is a tale worth telling for all that and I will tell it from
the inside; not as an interested observer or an envious admirer,
but as one who has been through the hoop and can claim, without
any boastfulness or exaggeration, to have lived through the years
of relentless driving, of days and nights at sea when man pits
himself against the elements, not for fun or bravado, but for his
very existence and for the existence of his home and his family.
And it is a cruel and bitter fight.

But there must be many folk who do not even know what a
sailing barge is and have certainly never seen one; so I must first
enlarge upon the impression they will have gained from the
illustrations in these pages.

There are, roughly, two sorts of sailing barges—coasting
barges and river barges, or, to be more explicit, big 'uns and little
'uns. Some of the later coasting barges such as were built in the
nineteen-twenties were, as barges go, colossal things with steel
hulls and capable of carrying 280 tons to sea and over 300 on a
river freight. They could trade up and down London river like
any of the small craft, or could slam their way down Channel or
northward to the Humber. In fact, they were quite worthy to ply
with safety any of the waters of the Home Trade, that is the
coasts of Great Britain and Ireland, the Isle of Man and the
Continental coast from Brest to the Elbe. All this with a crew of
three, generally two men and a boy. Four would not have been
too many, but, apart from the lowering of freightage rates, it was

difficult to obtain men and boys willing to go into sail when it was so much easier and more remunerative to go into motor and steam ships.

A more average size for a coasting barge is about 150 - 180 tons burden and a crew of two or three. Not three strapping fellows such as you get in fishing boats, but more often an old man and a couple of whippersnappers. It's a job to get mates, as I have already remarked, but some of the nippers one gets are by no means to be despised, for they would put many a husky liner bo'sun to shame when it comes to sculling a small boat in a tideway, running off heaving lines, setting sails and mooring up craft.

But more about barges themselves. Their flat lines are ugly and shapeless to a schooner man's eye but have a beauty of their own when you get used to them. Instead of a keel they are fitted with lee-boards which lower down on each side to prevent the barge from being blown to leeward when she is beating against the wind. The barge 'lays' on her leeboard and is thus pressed forward by her canvas instead of being blown broadside. There is a great art in using these leeboards and no barge is any good without them, not even the old boomies which were rigged with gaffs and booms and built with a deeper draft.

The great utility of a sailing barge is its combination of large capacity for cargo with exceedingly light draft (due to the flat bottom) and small crew.

A coaster can carry about 180 tons and only draw about seven feet six of water, not counting of course the depth to which the leeboards go. And when she is empty she will float in three feet of water. This means that she can carry cargoes up shallow creeks and rivers, load and discharge aground without heeling over, take short cuts across sand and mud banks which would be suicide for any other type of vessel: and on top of all that still do the deeper water work at sea. There was never a craft like them, and no wonder they are the only sailing vessels to hold their own against motor and steam in days when masts and spars are things of the past.

I suppose that one day they will, like many other beautiful ships of sail, disappear from our rivers and coasts, but they will hang on just as long as skippers and mates can be found.

Barges are given a lofty spread of canvas set upon heavy

spars which can all be lowered down for going under bridges. The mainmast does not go down through the deck and rest in a step in the keelson as in most sailing vessels. It has a rounded heel and stands in an iron mastcase on the deck. This case is open on the after side to allow the mast to be lowered by means of a threefold wire tackle on the forestay.

The distinguishing feature of a barge's spars is the sprit (which bargemen pronounce 'spreet') and this serves to hold up the peak of the mainsail. The upper end of the sprit is supported by the headrope of the sail and the heel by what is called a stanliff, a term which probably originated as standing lift. This consists of a rigging wire up to the hounds, where a collar goes round the mast, and at the lower end there is a big shackle to go into an iron band on the sprit. An iron muzzle goes round the mast to hold the heel of the sprit in position.

Once the angle and height of the sprit has been adjusted to suit the cut of the mainsail and topsail (an operation which requires considerable judgement and skill) it is not altered. The mainsail is stowed by means of brails to the mast. The topsail goes up the topmast on hoops and is sheeted out to the upper end of the sprit.

The boltsprit, which is the proper name for a bowsprit which pivots on a bolt, can be hove up on end to be out of the way when the barge is in docks or harbours. When it is lowered down, either by means of slacking away on the fore topmast stay or the jibstay, according to the weight of the spar, a jib and jib topsail can be set on it. This gives the barge a yacht-like air and completes a fine spread of sail. Of course, the barge sails much better with the bolt-sprit jib set, but in rivers and close waters bargemen generally keep their craft down to an inboard rig of topsail, mainsail, foresail and mizzen. A staysail can be set from the stem to the topmast head in light weather with the boltsprit steeved up out of the way.

Men who have always sailed under this spritsail rig swear there is none to beat it, but mostly they are men whose passage-making has been limited to reasonably smooth water. The boom rigged barges used to go much farther afield and their rig was by far the more suitable for heavy weather and long sea passages. The boomies were much the same as their spritty sisters in many respects except that the mainsail was set on a gaff and boom and lowered down when not in use. The first advantage of the boom sail is that in heavy weather it can be reefed and 'set smart', as they say, whereas the sprit sail can only be reduced by hauling on the brails. This completely ruins the set of the sail and spoils its driving power.

It is futile for sailors to argue as to which is the best sail, because each was designed for different conditions. But for handiness with a small crew the spritsail is the best that has been thought out after several hundred years of trial and error. In a small spritty barge a reasonably strong lad can stow up a mainsail while the skipper continues to manoeuvre the vessel under topsail and foresail.

And that's another thing; you can't keep your topsail set in a boomie once the mainsail is off her. What is more, the spritty bargeman, when negotiating a narrow creek or berthing alongside a wharf with the mainsail brailed up out of the way, has a clear vision to leeward.

A barge lacks the lovely curves of the round-bottomed schooners and ketches from the Channel and West Coast, but it is surprising what speed can be got out of her box-like hull. The speed and handiness of most barges depends (apart from their spread of canvas) upon the run aft. Barges built with an eye to racing such as the *Sara, Veronica* and *Princess,* have a run sloping up from almost amidships, but of course this tends to spoil the carrying capacity of the after hold.

Most barges are built of oak, pitch-pine and elm and are comfortable ships to live in. The cabins are invariably panelled and it is the pride and joy of bargemen to keep them scrupulously scrubbed and polished. After long and arduous hours on deck in winter time it is a great comfort to go down to a clean, orderly and homelike cabin.

A number of barge firms have had steel and iron vessels built, and these have the great advantage of eliminating the excessive use of pumps, especially in bad weather. This alters considerably the general strategy of the master, because in an 'iron pot', as such vessels are called, he can 'give it to her' in strong winds and rough water without fear of wetting his cargo. The man in a wooden barge has to consider the effects of strain upon his vessel in bad weather, which might open up a leak.

If an iron pot has good spars, sails and rigging and reliable ground tackle (anchors and chains) she can make passages in weather which would not be attempted in a wooden barge; especially if the latter is getting on in years, as most of them are these days. I have been in four steel barges for periods varying from six months to six years and never once have I had to ship a pump in them, though I have seen a lot of salt water across the main hatches and there have been times when I wondered whether the barge was on the water or under it.

Iron pots are uncomfortable ships to live aboard. They are either too hot or too cold down below. Clothes and bedding become damp and unhealthy. For these reasons many of the older bargemen will not go to sea in anything but wooden vessels.

An excellent impression of the shape of a barge's hull can be gained by Mr. Archie White's illustrations. For many years Mr. White has spent his spare hours sailing his yacht on the East Coast in company with the barges and I can vouch for the accuracy of the details. Wooden barges are fastened with trenails and spikes. The planking is 'rabbitted' so that no caulking is required in the sides. In iron and steel barges the construction is, of course, on much the same principle as that of any other vessel.

Now to more spicy matters, and I will tell you of a typical trip when I was mate of the *Oxygen*. She was a wooden barge which had once been used for carrying oil (hence her dreadful name) but since the advent of the motor tankers had been converted to the transport of general cargo. I believe that there had originally been three tank barges—the *Oxygen,* the *Hydrogen* and the *Nitrogen.*

I served in her for nearly two years under various skippers until she came under the command of an Essexman from Pin Mill named Percy Quantrill. He was a carefree, happy-go-lucky character, who had the great quality of taking all the dullness out of hard work and making the job seem like one long holiday. Enterprising and intelligent, he practically doubled the barge's earnings while he was in charge, and his never-failing sense of humour and goodheartedness alleviated all hardships. From the day he joined the barge at Sittingbourne we became fast friends.

Chapter Two

THE SKIPPER AND I stood before the bar in the Trafalgar at Erith and regarded, rather mournfully, the pint glasses which stood before us. They were not empty for they contained that inch of beer which entitled one to linger a little longer on the premises.

Percy fumbled in his pocket and produced a few coppers.

"I've got enough for the phone and another half pint each. The old man said ring up at twelve. It's about time we got orders."

The necessary fourpence rattled on the counter and brought the pasty-faced potman shuffling along the bar.

"Two halves in these."

We demolished the meagre measure (again with the exception of the last inch) and Percy went across the road to phone the owners. For a week the *Oxygen* had lain idle to her anchor off Erith, where empty barges are wont to bring up because it is good holding ground, generally well sheltered and also within a handy sail from any dock or wharf in the river.

A week's idleness is not too bad, but more than that generally imposes a financial strain on the crew. Master and mate receive no payment when they are without a cargo. They work by the share. The owner takes half the freightage and the crew the other half. For his part the owner pays for the upkeep and insurance of the barge and usually fixes the cargoes. The crew work the vessel, keep her in good order, paint her up in the summer, and always have her ready to load any type of cargo.

When work is slack the crew remain on board, hoping from day to day for orders to load, and generally looking after the barge. In their own interest, as well as that of the owner, they will not neglect the vessel or allow her to come to any damage by dragging her anchor, parting her moorings or lying in the way of other craft; because if they did, and orders came along, they might lose a freight. I have been aboard a barge anchored in the river for as long as six weeks without earning a cent, but that is a risk the sailor-man has to take when working a vessel on the share system. But owners are not so hard-hearted that they would let their bargemen sit aboard and starve, and they generally find them a job on the shipyard or something to keep the wolf from the cabin door.

Of all barge owners, probably the brothers Everard ("Bill" and "Fred" to sailormen) have done most to keep in being the last fleet of sail in face of competition from power-driven vessels. This in spite of the fact that they own a large number of motor ships themselves. Brought up as shipwrights, they have both built barges and still have a soft spot for them even in these tearaway days of speed and power.

Percy and I, being neither thrifty nor careful when in pocket, were feeling the pinch after a week at Erith. But all was well this time. Percy came back with a twinkle in his merry blue eyes and I could tell that he had got orders.

"We're for Ipswich. Full freight of barley in the Surrey dock."

We drank up and hurried down to the jetty where our boat was moored and got aboard without any delay. The barge was wanted alongside the steamship ready for the morning's work and it was already flood tide so we had no time to spare.

Once on board we went straight to the windlass and started to heave in the chain. There were eighteen fathoms of it in the water, but it came up easily because the wind was down-river and blew the barge up to her anchor over the flood. A sailing barge's windlass is powerful, simple and efficient, and I doubt if anything more suitable could be devised for a two-handed vessel. One firm's big coasters were given new-fangled patent contraptions when first built, but they had soon to be taken out and replaced by the old type.

As soon as the anchor was broken out the skipper went to the wheel and I set the foresail to blow us clear of a couple of barges lying outside us. Percy helped me get the topsail sheet out and we hoisted away on the halliard. He then nipped aft again to the wheel, steadied her helm and set the mizzen as the barge luffed across the river between two steamboats. In the meantime I got the topsail tack hard down and hove the anchor right up to the stem head. It was foul with a turn of the chain round the stock and another round the fluke, but there was no time to worry about that. The mainsail had got to be set and I let go the 'peaks, middles and lowers' which are the small brails used for stowing the sail. I stood by the main brail, which is of wire and works on a crab winch, until the skipper should give me the order. We would have had time to set the mainsail before we reached the other side of the river but we were on the port tack which meant that the sail would be pressed against the sprit and hard to sheet home. So Percy waited until he was ready to wind her and when he had pulled the wheel down to come about he ran along the main hatches, picked up the huge mainsheet block and called for me to let go the brail.

As the barge came up into the wind and the sail, now released of all its brails, unfolded itself he hooked the block on to the iron ring (called a traveller) which ran on the main horse. The main horse is a massive piece of oak which stretches across the barge's quarter-deck and is fastened securely so as to take the full weight of the sail. The traveller goes across the deck on the main horse each time the sails come over for a tack or gybe.

I believe it is a fact that all main horses are built three inches further forward on the starboard side than the port, to allow for the sprit being slung on the starboard side of the mainmast. But that is a technical detail for argument among the experts.

By the time the block was hooked the barge was head to wind and the canvas all ashake. To make the work as easy as possible I ran aft and sheeted home the sail before it should fill with wind on the other tack. This done, I let go the fore bowline, by which the foresail is held in the weather rigging to push the vessel's head round and also to prevent the canvas from flogging when head to wind.

We were off now under all plain sail—mainsail, topsail, foresail and mizzen—three thousand five hundred square feet of heavy red-ochred canvas which had all been set by two men in five minutes.

Now I had time to clear the anchor in case we should need to let it go unexpectedly, for in the river among thick traffic and in a strong tide one must be prepared for all eventualities. A steamship rounding-round head to tide, an eddy wind under the lee of a factory or an enforced tack when there is not sufficient room may all mean that the anchor is the only means of keeping the barge out of collision and avoiding damage.

Once the anchor had been cleared we were able to fetch up through Halfway Reach, and Percy called for the big staysail to

be set on the topmast stay, as the wind was flukey when we were
between the built-up areas near Dagenham and Barking.

Once we narrowly missed a little Conyer brick barge standing
to cross our head on the starboard tack. Now we, being on the
port tack, should have given way to the other vessel—that is,
according to Article 17 of the International Rules for the
Prevention of Collision at Sea. But Percy was a bargeman and
much too much of an individual to be pinned down by hidebound
rules and regulations. He kept the *Oxygen* full-and-by so that we
crossed the bows of the other barge by a matter of feet, and as the
brickman, also holding to his course, swept under our stern I had
to shorten our boat's painter to avoid its being cut adrift. Neither
skipper turned a hair or said a word—not aloud anyway. What
each said under his breath is another matter.

I was surprised at Percy cutting things so fine when he was on
the wrong tack, for his judgement in the river was generally
pretty good. So I ventured to ask him why he had not put about to
give the other man a clean board. His answer would have come
as rather a shock to the pundits of the International Convention.
He shook his head wisely and gave me this advice.

'Never give way to a Kentishman.'

'Why not?' I innocently asked.

'`Cos he'll never give way to you.'

And there the incident, and the discussion thereon, was finally
closed. On the next tack the two barges were well clear of each
other and the *Oxygen* could stand across to the weather shore of
Gallion's Reach.

There has for years been a keen rivalry, and in some cases
almost enmity, between the Kentish bargemen from the Medway
waters—by which I mean men from Sittingbourne, Gillingham,
Strood, Chatham, Conyer, and Queenborough—and those from
the Essex and Suffolk side who generally hail from Ipswich, Pin
Mill, Mistley, Burnham, or the banks of the numerous Essex
creeks. This rivalry originated, as far as I am able to trace, in the
heyday of sailing barges many years ago when Kentishmen
consented to sail for lower freights than the Essexmen and as a
result there was a general reduction. But no doubt geography also
played its part in setting one lot against the other because,
although rivalry is almost unnoticeable among the crews when

they are ashore together, it is in deadly earnestness when they are under way.

The Essexmen always pride themselves that they keep up their ships better and sail them better and it is a fact that on the whole the Essex and Suffolk craft do look a lot smarter. But this is largely due to the fact that they are generally carrying clean cargoes such as wheat, maize, oats, bran, midlings, rice meal, flour—all of which is generally referred to as the corn work.

On the other hand the Kentishman, apart from working on the dirtier shore, often has his vessel lying under the lee of the many cement works which cover him with a white dust. Also he frequently carries such cargoes as coal, mud ballast, cement, and even London garbage (a revolting load which is politely known as 'rough stuff'). But perhaps the worst element he has to contend with in keeping his barge up to scratch is the discolouring properties of the silt and water in some of the Kentish creeks. I have lain two tides in Milton Creek, near Sittingbourne and watched my fresh, shining black paint turn a sickly, uncertain purple and lovely white enamel go a blotchy grey. Other colours are similarly ruined and even well-kept ironwork is disfigured. This, combined with the effect of a particularly adhesive and evil smelling mud all over the barge's sides, makes her look as though she hasn't had a paint up or a scrub round for months.

The appearance of the Essex barges is also enhanced by the fact that they more often carry boltsprits (bowsprits) than the Kentishmen, and this certainly gives them a more seamanlike bearing. The Kentish barges haven't the need for them as they don't get a long reach like the Essexmen bound down-swin. Trips along the Kent shore are generally shorter and the crews need a handy inboard rig. Moreover, they do the greater part of the work up through the bridges of London, and under such bridges as Rochester and Maidstone. This entails frequent lowering of the masts and gear and in such operations a boltsprit is a thundering nuisance.

But as far as sailoring is concerned I don't think there is anything to chose between a good Essexman and a good Kentishman. When the races are held in the summer (there are two races each year) the Kentish barges have always been just as well sailed and as deftly handled as those from the Essex shore.

Perhaps the only difference is that the Essexman takes his sailing very seriously and works his crew tremendously hard, whereas the Kentishman treats racing with an air of light-hearted confidence.

Now to return to the *Oxygen* and the incident which caused me to digress thus far. We got well clear of the Conyer barge and fetched into the lee of Beckton Gas Works.

We had a clear tack through Gallions as far as the wind was concerned, but the Albert Dock was locking in, and a host of tugs, lighters and sailing barges were rounding round athwart the tide to get in there. To further block our path two large steamships were anchored in the middle of the river, waiting to go into the King George at high water, so that we were forced well over to leeward and had to make a quick tack to get clear of the eddy tide in the bight by Woolwich Arsenal.

The next stretch was Woolwich Reach, long and narrow, with its banks lined by factory after factory and miles of lighter roads which further reduce the room for manoeuvre. From here to the Surrey Dock, which opens into Limehouse Reach, was the trickiest part of our journey. The tide ran hard, especially in the bight formed by the junctions of Blackwall Reach and Bugsby's Reach and where Greenwich Reach meets Blackwall.

Under sail among big steamboats, coasters, tugs and other sailormen, the judgement of the skipper has to be very accurate. There is no changing of a decision once made or his vessel will soon be swept foul of someone, or else he will have to let go his anchor in a hurry and find he is in a position from which he cannot get under way again until the tide turns or eases, which might mean that he would miss the lock-in at the dock where he is bound and perhaps lose his freight altogether. This would also involve some disorganisation at the ship from which his cargo is being unloaded because, if he is not there in time to take it in from overside, it would have to be landed into a P.L.A. warehouse with considerable expense to those concerned. So you see, there are a lot of important factors depending on whether the skipper spins his helm down at the right moment or the wrong one. And the co-ordination and foresight of the mate are of great help to the man at the wheel.

As we came sweeping round the bend into Limehouse Reach

the wind came more abeam and Percy edged her to one side of
the river so that a Norwegian ship coming down river could not
get between us and the Surrey dock. The Norwegian blew his
whistle and held his course because, except for our barge, he
would have had a clear course. The traffic was thicker on our
starboard hand and in the middle of the river. But had he come
between us and the dock-head we should have been carried past
our destination by the flood tide and probably missed the lock-in,
so we held our luff and hoped that the other fellow would shift
his helm.

Had he not done so he would have cut us in two, but Percy's
nerve was the steadier and the ship blew port and passed close
under our stern to the accompaniment of much swearing from the
bridge. Percy had his hands full to get our barge to the dock-
head, but with his usual breezy naïveté called back over his
shoulder:

'Oh, to Hell with yer. You've got more steam than we have,
haven't you?'

Which, I think, effectively proved to the Norwegian that he
was wrong for, although steam does not always give way to sail
in London River, we at least had the law on our side.

'Pick up your mainsail', Percy shouted as we luffed athwart
the tide, and I hove as fast as I could on the main brail and
middles and lowers as he let go the sheet.

Percy steadied the helm and then nipped to the main horse
again and unhooked the block.

'All yours.'

I got the mainsail off her in time to let go the foresail halliards
as we shot in under topsail towards a crowd of lighters waiting to
dock.

'Down topsail. Slack your anchor down.'

The reason for slackening the anchor chain was that in the
river a barge's anchor is always carried over the stem head ready
to let go at a moment's notice, with three turns round the barrel
of the windlass. When going alongside there is often a risk of the
anchor fluke damaging other craft or possibly sticking into our
own bow, so sufficient chain is slackened to allow the anchor to
swing underneath the barge's forefoot. There it can do no harm
to anyone.

It is a pity that big power ships with stockless patent anchors

housed in the bows don't sometimes do likewise. Most steamboat
sailors never seem to think of it and there have been times when
their anchors have caused quite a bit of damage.

As we came gently alongside I dropped the bowline of our
horseline over the dolly of a large lighter which was waiting,
with many others, to lock in. As I did so Percy topped up the
mizzen boom and locked the wheel amidships. The *Oxygen* had
arrived.

We then stowed everything up properly and waited for the
lock gates to open.

By the time we got through the locks an hour later the lower
part of the dock was chock-o-block with craft of all sorts, but
mostly lighters. Those entering the dock could not get through
and those coming out from the various wheat and timber docks
which are connected to the large Greenland Dock (the nucleus of
the Surrey dock system) were arrested by the advance of the
incomers. By the time all our lot had locked in there was a
hopeless jam-up and no one could move. I wondered where the
much vaunted organisation of the Port of London Authority came
in. But the pleasure trippers who are taken in launches round the
P.L.A. docks are spared such sights as these.

Some of the lightermen, seeing the hopelessness of the
confusion, caught a turn with their headropes on the nearest
bollard and bolted for home. This, of course, did not help people
like ourselves who had to find a way through the crush somehow
and get alongside a ship at the top end of the dock ready to take
in cargo in the morning.

It was a hard sweat, running a heaving line ahead when we
saw the chance, making a few yards of progress now and then at
the cost of tremendous effort. Often we had to shift and re-moor
abandoned lighters or help other men shift their craft so that we
could move ourselves.

In the midst of all this chaos it took us two hours to progress a
quarter of a mile. And in these circumstances the Greenland is
not nearly so bad as the Albert Dock basin, where sometimes the
jam-up is literally hopeless and P.L.A. tugs have to be sent for to
clear up the mess.

Although the wind was dead against us we could not get a tug
because we were told that none was available. All the P.L.A. tugs

were busy docking and undocking big ships on the high water and clearing such confusions as that we had just survived.

Some of the hardest work I have ever done in my life has been in the docks of the Port of London and many are the curses I have rained upon bridgemen who won't open bridges; tugmen who won't tow you (especially if it's near their knocking-off time); lightermen who cast off your rope without warning. Here and there we find P.L.A. men with a soft spot for sailormen (as all barges are called in the London River) but they are few and far between. Perhaps our best pal has always been a fine old character called 'Nobby', the foreman at the South West India Dock. He, more than anyone else, always sees to it that the sailorman keeps clear of damage and Nobby provides all the help he can.

Bless your old heart, Nobby. You may not know me from Adam, but more than once you have gone to a bit of extra trouble that has saved me many a hard heave when I have been dog tired after sleepless nights at sea.

So much for the docks. They are no haven of refuge for a sailorman. All they represent to us is a damned lot of hard work until the barge is finally loaded and out in the river again. Once in the tideway the bargeman is again his own master.

Chapter Three

THE NEXT DAY we loaded. Amid an almost unbelievable hubbub, the ear-splitting rattle of the ship's donkey engines, the whine of the electric cranes on the quay, the swearing and shouting of the dockees and lightermen, the bags of barley, eight or ten at a time, came thumping down into our hold.

There they were seized almost savagely by the perspiring stowers and laid fore and aft in the barge as closely as possible so as not to waste any space. These stowers are paid by piece work—that is, the more tonnage they stow the more they earn—and from their point of view it doesn't matter a damn how it is stowed as long as it is out of the ship and aboard the barge. But the skipper of the barge has a right to see that his vessel is loaded in a proper manner so that she is in good seaworthy trim and so that the cargo will not shift.

So there is a constant war being waged between the skipper and the stowers. Percy would pace up and down the deck swearing and bluffing, saying that he had never seen such stowing in all his born days, that he would stop the job and call the shipworker if they didn't shove 'em under the wings better, that by the time they'd finished there would be more barley above the coamings than below, that the people who stow barges ought to bloody-well go to sea in 'em and that, generally speaking, their work was a damned disgrace.

And then a dockee would flare back and want to know, in his own method of expression which included a constant repetition of a word I cannot repeat here, who the hell the skipper thought he was talking to, that they didn't want sailormen in the dock, that they were a bloody nuisance to everyone, and that if the skipper could stow these blank bags any better he could blank blank well come and do it his blank self, and that he could go and blank himself and that he didn't want the blank job anyway, so blank it.

And that more or less represents a slight argument between a bargeman and a dockee, the result of which would be precisely nothing. But you have got to keep on at them to get any sort of decent stowage or else they'll think you're soft and drop them in anywhere.

After all that one of them looked up at me and winked and muttered, 'Gawd blimey, I bet he's a nice old sod to sail with.'

But Percy knew his job and he knew dockees.

Occasionally, of course, all this swearing and counter-swearing (which is known by the delightful term of 'dockology') does lead to a scrap. Once I saw the mate of a Rochester barge jump down into the hold and set about a dockee with such vicious intent that there was a hold up of work to witness the flow of blood. The mate was a strong country lad who had been made as hard as nails by years of barging, and the poorly built Cockney, for all his spirit and courage, was nowhere in it.

Then the skipper gave the mate a severe wigging because he had laid out a stower, thereby reducing the gang to three, which meant that the barge would not finish loading in time to catch the high water lock and might lose a lovely fair wind that was blowing down the river.

All that is dock life and in time one grows to be part and parcel of it.

By late afternoon we were loaded, taking a stack three bags high in the main hatchway and one bag high forward. We had to heave our way out from the side of the ship through a mass of lighters which were clustered around her and round the overlap of lighters waiting on the next ship along the quay. By five o'clock, when the dockers knocked off and all the unholy din melted away into a blessed peace, we found a quiet spot to complete covering up and get ready for sea.

The stack has to be covered over and made proof from rain or sea by means of tarpaulins. Bargemen are expert at battening down and putting on lashings, but for two men it is hard work, for the cloths are heavy and the tiniest drain of water from a sea or rain shower might ruin many pounds worth of corn. I will say for sailormen that they are very conscientious in the care of their cargoes, provided the owners give them the proper sized cloths and lashings to do the job and do not skimp things for the sake of cheapness as is sometimes the case, relying on the crews' ingenuity to keep the cargo dry.

We finished our work about eight o'clock that night and next morning I had to turn out at daylight to get the vessel scrubbed round and shipshape while the skipper nipped up to London to get his Customs clearance, Bills of Lading and (very important) a 'sub' on the freight. Captains are always allowed an advance of money for ship's and crews' expenses during the voyage.

Now there were two barges which loaded the same time as us named the *Doris* and the *Kimberley.* Without diving into personal differences or ancient rivalries, I'll say that Percy would put to sea in any weather within reason at any time of the day or night, irrespective of the amount of work involved or subsequent lack of sleep, to beat the skipper of the *Kimberley.* And the *Kimberley* as well as the *Doris* was bound to Ipswich like ourselves. That is one reason why we worked late that night getting ready for sea so that the *Kimberley* should not have a start on us in the morning. We didn't worry about the *Doris,* as her skipper was generally regarded as a decent old stick who went about his business quietly and efficiently in his own way and made his passages with a steady regularity. But the skipper of the *Kimberley* was on the boastful side and, as far as I could tell from his conversation, had but little respect for the younger generation of bargemen. And in this respect the younger bargemen reciprocated.

Our self-imposed overtime availed us but little, for the following day the wind flew into the north-west and blew a proper 'spoondrifter'. In fact, instead of undocking and getting away down the river we all had to set to work putting out extra moorings to prevent the barges being blown adrift in the dock. Even a big steamer under tow up the dock became unmanageable in one of the wildest squalls and came charging down on top of the craft broadside on. Luckily the damage done was slight, except for breaking adrift a number of lighters which were in turn blown across the dock like a herd of cattle in panic.

The next day was Sunday and the weather had fined The wind was backing and veering between north and north-west and Percy decided to get down the river on the afternoon tide. Seeing us heaving down towards the lock gates the *Doris* and the *Kim berley* also let go their moorings and we all three locked out together. While we were in the lock waiting for the level of the water to be lowered to that of the river outside the three skippers discussed the weather and the prospects of the voyage before us.

'Don't think much on't,' said the skipper of the *Doris,* glancing skywards as he checked his stern rope. 'Wind's too far no'th'ly. And that breeze we had yesterday ain't done yet. She'll come again afore long, mark my words.'

'Gawd, yes,' broke in the master of the *Kimberley*, 'way the wind is now they 'ont fetch Blackwall Reach—and if they 'ont fetch Blackwall they 'ont fetch Harwich.'

'Blust me,' chipped in Percy in his sing-song Suffolk, 'you're bright and bloody cheerful ain't you. I know one barge that'll go down along somewhere this tide, what say you, Mister Mate? You ain't got a gal hereabouts have you? And the beer's not all that wonderful to keep us lingering.'

So with this differing of opinion the *Doris* and the *Kimberley* came to their anchors just above the dock-head in Limehouse Reach while the foolhardy *Oxygen* spread her wings and went 'blaring off all hell and no notion', as the critical ancients are wont to say of the younger generation.

As the skipper of the *Kimberley* had foretold, we could not fetch down Blackwall Reach and had to make two boards into the slack tide on the south shore to get round the point so that we could bear away for Bugsby's. But we were finished with windward work then and the mainsheet and vang were given a bit more drift to hump the old gal along a bit.

At nightfall we were well down past Gravesend, and the Ovens Buoy winked merrily at us as we squared off round it into the Lower Hope. Once this buoy is reached the worries of river work are done and in the broad Hope and Sea Reach the river banks get further and further apart until they break out into the unprotected estuary.

Now I am going to wander away from my tale again because the Ovens buoy always reminds me of one of the best known skippers who ever held a barge's wheel, the irrepressible Captain Enoch Hart, known in every port and pub between Yarmouth and the Isle of Wight as 'Knocker'. People have always remembered him by his loud laugh, his Cockney humour and his happy-go-lucky ways. Since boyhood his home has been London River and I have never yet met any sailorman who, like Knocker, could reel off without hesitation every one of the hundreds of wharves, docks and jetties, however small, in any part of the river. Nothing ever worried him, and he took good fortune and bad in the same happy way. As long as he had the price of a pint the world was worth living in and all was well. And, incidentally, as a connoisseur of pints of any brew, his judgement was acknowledged by all.

One dark night Knocker was driving up the Lower Hope in a calm, trying to get to Greenhithe on that tide so that he could have a night at home. Occasionally there were a few catspaws of wind from the west to help him keep control of the barge, but he was relying mainly on the strong spring flood to get him home. The mate took the wheel so that Knocker could be free to judge how the tide was taking her. And this is how he told us about it.

'I looks r'and the mains'l an' I sees the ole Ovens light there, goin' in an' aht, in an' aht, in an' aht. An' I says to the mate, "luff her a bit me ole cock if you get a puff," I keeps a 'lookin' r'and the mains'l and we're a-driving up fast right athwart and dead in line with the buoy. I didn't want to let go me anchor, bein' in so much water, but I'm wondering if we're goin' to clear that buoy. I keep poppin' me 'ead r'and the mains'l as we gets closer and closer and there she is, goin' in and aht, in an' aht, in an' aht—then we 'its it, and it goes *right* aht.'

The riverside would miss old Knocker. May you live to drink many more pints yet—like that eight in a row you polished off in the Rabbits one night for a bet. (Easy money for you, wasn't it?)

Now I'll go back to the *Oxygen* again and promise not to digress any more. I must confess to a common failing among sailormen when spinning a yarn; one thing reminds me of another and off I go again.

It blew hard that night and as we sailed down Sea Reach the wind was round about south-west and there was every indication of bad weather. The sun had gone down looking pale and greasy behind a wall of grey-black cloud and the lights were hard and bright. On such nights, when a southerly or south-westerly gale is coming, one can see fantastic distances in the estuary, and I have known in such circumstances the North Foreland light visible in the West Swin, twenty-five miles away.

There are something like seventy lights in the estuary to mark the many dangerous shoals and rocks and sand-banks. That night it seemed as though we could see the lot. I inwardly felt some satisfaction at being able to pick them out and name them without a chart—not that we had one anyway. But through sheer practice which comes of regular trading in one area it is possible to recognise lights covering hundreds of miles of coast.

Apart from the fact that they are all ingeniously arranged to flash 'twice every five seconds' or 'three every ten' and so on, each light has to the regular coaster an indefinable characteristic of its own. For instance, there are many lights on the Channel and East Coasts and the Thames Estuary, whose frequency I have never known but which I am always able to identify without hesitation. I do not know the timing of the occulting light on the South Shoebury buoy, but it always looks like someone solemnly pulling a face at you. Then the Ovens always has a quick cheerful wink like a wicked old man on the spree, and the Maplin Spit a sort of 'here I am' flash. They all seem to say something to the lonely bargeman who relies so much on them for his life and livelihood.

We looked dubiously at this array before us as we passed the Chapman Lighthouse and I asked Percy what he was going to do.

'Well,' he replied slowly, 'if we had any sense we'd bring up under the Yantlet. But I don't know as we have. I'm thinking that with this wind we could run the flood and be at the Spitway before high water, just right. And however hard it blows it's a fair wind. So what do you say. Shall we let her go?'

Percy always used to ask my opinion of the weather, but I do not think it ever made any difference to what he had already decided to do. It was just a sort of courtesy. So I said, 'Yes, let her rip. If we're not in Harwich to-morrow we'll be in Kingdom Come, so what the hell.'

We gave her a bit more main sheet, put an extra lashing on the boat in the davits, made sure all the wedges were tight, lashed down the ropes and gear on the hatches, fished the anchor well up, passed a gasket round the mizzen, set the weather backstay bar taut and put a preventer tackle on it, had a hot cup of cocoa, and went roaring down past Southend Pier like a steamboat. I daresay we were knocking off a good eight knots, which isn't bad for a deep-loaded barge with only about three inches freeboard amidships.

The water rushed along our lee decks and once or twice washed round the wheel but the old barge was safe enough provided nothing broke under the strain. She was well fitted out and we had faith in our gear aloft, which is half the battle in heavy weather. And another thing one must have in a gale of wind is a cool head and steady nerve at the wheel and a combination of guts and common sense forward.

But it is impossible to foresee every contingency, and who would have thought that a coat button should bring us dangerously near to disaster that night?

She took a bit of a root to windward, as any fore-and-aft-rigged ship is liable to, and Percy, in pushing the helm up to correct her, slipped on the deck and caught the front buttons of his jacket in one of the spokes. The barge bore up all right but a bit too far and just as Percy wanted to ease the wheel back again the spoke in his jacket prevented him; and being off his balance he could not get it free quick enough.

To our horror the barge kept bearing up until the wind was on

the other quarter and, with a thundering flogging of canvas and
crash of spars, she gybed. (To gybe means that the vessel has so
far run off her course that the wind has caught her on the other
quarter and blown all the sails and gear over on to the opposite
side.)

A gybe in a spritsail barge is a serious matter, and even in fine
weather is undertaken with great care so as not to snap the
topmast, bring the sprit down in halves or break the vangs. To
have the sprit and sails crash over unexpectedly from one side to
the other in a gale of wind on a dark night might mean a terrible
disaster.

The *Oxygen* shook and staggered as though she had struck a
rock at full tilt. I dashed along the weather deck as she gnawed
round into the wind and could see the topmast still standing but
bending over in a great arc. Percy was roaring to me to 'Down
topsail' and I let the halliards go with a run. He had got control of
the wheel again and was trying to get the barge before the wind
but she was stubborn in bearing away. The short, steep seas were
breaking right over the main hatches and the whole barge seemed
buried in a welter of foaming water.

As soon as the topsail head had run down and taken the
weight off the topmast I dodged round to the main brail-winch
and hove like hell to get part of the mainsail off her. By this time
Percy had got her before the wind again and shouted to me to
come aft. He wanted the lee vang set tight ready to gybe her back
on to her course.

Once this was done, the mainsail being brailed up as far as the
sprit, we were safe once more and gybed back. Not a thing had
parted and by a sheer miracle nothing had torn or come adrift. In
nine cases out of ten a barge gybing like that would have lost her
masts, sprit, canvas and all over the side; but some guardian
angel must have been looking after us that night.

My next job was to toil and sweat at the topsail halliards
again. Setting a barge's topsail in ordinary weather is no task for
a weakling and in a gale of wind it is more than enough for a
strong man. Percy could not leave the wheel, so slowly the sail
crept up the mast until it wanted another six or seven feet to be
set. Then I had to make fast and get my wind back. In spite of the
purchase I could not get that last bit up until I swung off the fore

hatches on the halliard fall and nipped a quick turn round the mast winch, Then, by heaving on the winch-handle with my left hand and holding the halliard with my right as it came off the barrel, I hove the headstick to the block aloft and made fast, a very blown and exhausted person.

The *Oxygen* ran along quite comfortably under topsail, foresail and half mainsail but, alas, there was no relief She was not going fast enough for us to catch our tide across the Spitway, and once more my tired arms and aching back had to go into battle again to pull the full mainsail out. Foot by foot the great bellying mass of red canvas unfolded itself until the sheet was half home. Then we let go the weather vang with a run so that the weight of wind was transferred to the sheet and out came the full mainsail. The barge surged forward again to resume her breakneck speed and we both gave vent to those oft-repeated thoughts—that crews of coasting barges need to be either bloody fools or horses. I once read a book about barges which said that they were 'easily handled by two men'. The word 'easily' might well have been left out.

We reached the Spitway in the early hours, somewhere about two o'clock in the morning, and had to gybe again because the wind had southered and the passage across the sands lies nearly north and south. This meant brailing the mainsail half up again and lowering the topsail so that once we were over the shallows and in the Wallet Channel all the business of getting the canvas on her had to be gone through once more. Percy did most of it this time as I happened to be taking my turn at the wheel.

As we ran down past Clacton, Frinton and Walton and rounded the Naze into the Medusa channel by the Stone Banks buoy the weather moderated, and by the time the lights of Harwich were beckoning us into the calm safety of its spacious harbour all our troubles were at an end. We had 'got our passage' and all that remained was to blow up the narrow Orwell River in quiet solitude, taking turns at the wheel and striving hard to keep our eyes open. Both of us were very tired but we knew that there was to be no rest or sleep for us for many hours yet.

As soon as Ipswich dock opened we had to heave her in and then set our topsail again to blow up the dock and round the corner at the top end to our discharging berth. By that time we had recovered from our sleepiness and set about mooring up and

stowing the sails before having a mighty breakfast of bacon and
eggs. Dinner in Surrey Dock and breakfast in Ipswich was not
bad going; and after our stomachs were full we set about
preparing to discharge. The dockees were ready for us and we
soon had the wedges out, lashings off, and the hatches cleared.

Percy then went home, for he lived at Pin Mill, a nearby
village which is one of the beauty spots of East Anglia. There
was not much left for me to do except shift hatches and carry
sixty gallons of fresh water aboard for the return journey. We
always filled up with water when the opportunity offered, for it is
a problem for a small vessel to do so in London River.

Two days later I phoned the pub at Pin Mill to tell Percy that
we were empty and ready for sea. There was a spanking
northerly wind, which was just what we wanted for a trip to
London, and while Percy was coming up from Pin Mill I shifted
down the dock with the help of the mate of another barge. Since
all barges are really sailed short-handed there is a genuine
camaraderie among the crews, and both skippers and mates are
always willing to lend each other a hand. They appreciate each
other's difficulties better than anyone else and know how much a
helping hand can mean.

Within a couple of hours we were bowling down the river
between those lovely wooded hills and lowering the boltsprit
ready to set a jib and jib-topsail to such a merry fair breeze.

Just as we ran down by Pin Mill we saw two barges struggling
painfully up to windward on the last of the tide, for they were too
far down river to catch the lock-in at Ipswich that day. The first
one proved to be the *Doris;* and we couldn't help a smug smirk
when we saw that the second was the worthy *Kimberley.*

We sailed close across her head as she winded, and Percy
could not resist singing out:

'What do you think of the weather, old skipper?' And, in my
turn, I could not resist adding:

'Too far no'therly, ain't it !'

Chapter Four

I DO NOT KNOW really why a trip to Snape should stick out in my memory after all these years I have been barging. Perhaps it was because Percy and I dissolved partnership there, for he left the *Oxygen* when we had discharged our barley alongside the old maltings. Or perhaps it was because from then on I left the ranks of barge-mate to be appointed to the hundred and ten tons *Hambrook* as her master, proudly joining her on the shipyard at Sittingbourne after sailing home in the *Oxygen* with her new skipper.

Or, then again, Snape may stand out in my musings because it is a back-of-beyond place belonging to a bygone age; a tiny, old fashioned village such as only Suffolk can boast. And perhaps not least, for our surprise at finding in so forsaken a spot such warm friendliness, lovable old country characters, remarkably pretty girls and such riotous times to be had.

Yes, if you are a bargeman, Snape is worth going to; but probably the touring visitor, who might even take these writings as a recommendation of the place, would as likely find it a dreary stretch of country road without even the compact beauty of many another antiquated English village. You must know the people first and then you will learn to know Snape.

We sailed out of the Royal Albert Dock with the *Phoenician* as company. She also was bound for Snape and her skipper was half owner of our barge. The *Phoenician* was the champion racing barge, a fast, specially built model with magnificent lee-boards, a beautifully standing spread of canvas and a long run aft to give her speed. There was not much chance of our beating her to Snape, but I thought Percy did remarkably well to keep her in full view all the way to Harwich. When we arrived off there the *Phoenician* was brought up on the Rolling Grounds and we went on into the harbour. Good spring tides are needed to get a loaded barge up the River Alde to Snape and, there being only one pilot available for the upper reaches, there was no object in both barges arriving there together and hindering each other. So the *Phoenician* went away down while we hung on a day or two at anchor off Shotley before sailing the few miles to Orford Haven, which is where the rivers Butley, Ore and Alde run into the sea.

It was a fine morning with a smart westerley breeze when we arrived off the Haven, the entrance to which is almost concealed from seaward. Being expected, the pilot came off to us in his little white boat after we had jilled about for a short time, and we sailed in towards him and backed the foresail again while he got aboard.

He was an old man with white hair surmounted by a smart cheese-cutter cap. He greeted us with a sort of Victorian correctness.

'Good morning, Master, good morning, Mr. Mate. I hope you have had a good passage. Will you please slack my boat astern, Mr. Mate? I'll take the wheel now, if you please, and we'll steer for that patch of broken water. Does she bear up well, Master?'

Percy assured him that she would bear up as well as most barges, but as a precaution the old man had me stand by the main brail to get the mainsail off her in case she would not turn quickly enough before the wind in the narrow entrance.

It is a hazardous place to enter at any time, but fortunately with a westerly wind touching off the land everything was in our favour. Once in the entrance, where the tide swirls and breaks among the shifting knolls of sand, a barge *must* go in, as the strength of the ingoing stream is phenomenal.

The old *Oxygen* bore up without hesitation and made a smart right angle turn as her nose almost touched the beach. The old pilot dropped smartly into his boat, warning us to keep clear of a shoal a little farther on. But after she bore up she gnawed up into the wind against her helm (as barges often do) and with a jolt we hit the shingle.

In any place but Orford Haven, with the possible exception of the neighbouring river at Bawdsey, the barge would have lost way and stopped. Instead she rose a good foot out of the water and scored over the shingle with the aid of the swift tide and her own speed. Before we knew what we were about she was in deep water again and tearing up the river at a breakneck rate of something like fourteen knots over the ground. It's a good thing the river here is straight because the old *Oxygen* would have been a bit of a problem on a corner at that speed.

Only a strip of shingle beach separates the river from the North Sea until some four or five miles up, where the seaman gets the rather weird sensation of passing inside Orfordness Lighthouse.

The tide eases after the first bend, and we settled down to a pleasant sail as far as the Aldeburgh brickfield, where we anchored to await the river pilot. The tides had not been as good as expected and we could see the *Phoenician* some miles ahead being taken up to Snape. She must have arrived before there was enough water on the berth at the maltings.

We sampled the social life of Aldeburgh, which meant finding a cheerful pub and sticking to it, and one day walked across country to Snape. It was about four miles, and we trod the ancient path known as the Sailors' Walk. Apparently in years gone by sailing vessels used to do just as we had done, anchor at the back of Aldeburgh and wait for water to Snape. The crews used to walk up through the private estates, by the tolerance of the landowners, to sample Snape ale at the Plough and Sail. This path has been known as Sailors' Walk for much longer than living memory and is still looked upon as a privileged right of way to seafaring men.

When we came back the pilot was waiting and also another man with a motor-boat. This motor-boat was not powerful enough to tow the barge but assisted her by pulling her head this way and that to negotiate the sharp turns and avoid the multitudinous mud banks.

The pilot and the motor-boat man were a strange pair. The pilot was a tall youngish fellow with bright blue eyes, a hawk nose and big gold earrings. For all the world he might have been a buccaneer stepped straight out of history. The other was a heavy, dour individual with his eye on the money and not exactly a bargeman's friend. The funny thing about them was that the pilot knew where the deepest water was but could not handle a sailing vessel, whereas the motor-boat man could steer a sailing vessel but did not know where the water was. So they worked by the pilot signalling to the motor-boat whether to go straight ahead or pull the barge's head port or starboard and at the same time telling the skipper, who held the wheel, which way to go and what set of tide to allow for.

At first the system seemed very far from infallible. The pilot

said heave the anchor up, the motor-boat broke down, the barge
cast herself on the wrong tack and we finished up ashore on the
mud. Percy and I were then left to our fate, and it took us all the
next tide to lay off our big second anchor on a wire hawser and
heave her off into deep water again.

It was an unfortunate day altogether, for I slipped on the deck
and dropped the dinner overboard and Percy was worried stiff
because he had not been able to get any money to send home to
his wife, although he had a cheque for the freight. Finally we
rowed ashore and walked into Aldeburgh and after a lot of
trouble got the cheque cashed: but on the way back in the pitch
black darkness and thick fog misfortune overtook us again.

Percy was happy again now that he had posted the money off
home and was singing some of his hymns. He knew miles of
them. Just as we were trying to pick our way through the deserted
brickfield, arm in arm for safety's sake, he struck up 'Lead,
Kindly Light', and at the conclusion of the first verse we
suddenly descended into black space and landed with a sickening
thud at the bottom of a fifteen foot hole lined with bricks. I was
unhurt but Percy sprained his ankle badly and it was some time
before we could hoist ourselves out.

The next day the pilot and his accomplice came aboard once
more and this time operations were more successful and we
wound our way tediously up to the berth at Snape, the
Phoenician having discharged and come down.

While we were there Percy, who could not see eye to eye with
the owners of the barge over money matters, decided to pack his
bag and clear out. After a night's farewell celebration, in which
nearly all the village joined us, we bid each other good-bye
outside the Plough and Sail. We had been a perfect team, Percy
and I, and good friends into the bargain. We had sailed hard and
had good times ashore, and with his leaving my interest in the
Oxygen began to fade. But I made many a stout friend while
waiting for the new skipper to arrive and even after all these
years I can picture very vividly those evenings in the bar-parlour
of the Plough and Sail, the place shaped like a ship's cabin in
which we all sat round the one table, taking it in turns on
Saturday nights to give a step dance or a song. My old accordion
was in great demand on these occasions and I was ably helped

out by an old villager with a fiddle. (It it amazing how people who make their own amusement can have a far jollier and more uproarious time than any of your lovers of London who have to pay out large sums from their earnings for someone to entertain them with something which in the end they may not approve of.)

The new skipper of the *Oxygen* came down from Ipswich, having been promoted from one of the firm's smaller barges, and brought the news that I was to take charge of the *Hambrook* on our return to London River. He had another mate joining him there.

So ended my one and only trip to Snape. The new skipper was an enterprising young fellow, not given to dallying, and we were away the next day to Orford. We were not strangers to each other by any means and I liked him well enough, for he was possessed of that cheerfulness and casual generosity which I have never found so evident in any class or society as among the sailing bargemen of the East Coast. Nowhere else have I seen a hard-earned guinea given away without so much as a thought or hours of gruelling work endured to help someone in difficulty.

It was not surprising, therefore, that Nobby (that was his name) would take no money from me for my food on the passage home, lent me some cash to 'set up home' in the *Hambrook's* cabin, and gave me one or two valuable wrinkles on a skipper's dealings with owners and brokers.

So I left him at Erith and he and a crowd of other skippers wished me luck in the Trafalgar tavern as I set off to take over my new ship.

Chapter Five

I WAS NO NOVICE at joining strange ships in the dark and when I reached Sittingbourne town I purchased three candles, a frying-pan, a pound of sausages and a loaf of bread. In my bag there were also a blanket and an extra jersey. These were the essentials of life until the next morning, no matter in what state I found the cabin, and the only thing left to chance was the wherewithal to make a fire and fry the sausages. And since the *Hambrook* was on the shipyard and probably smothered in shipwright's shavings there was not much doubt about cooking facilities.

Before proceeding down the long lane to the waterside I deemed it good strategy to call in at the White Hart. Here, where I was not entirely unknown, I soon found myself talking to a shipwright who had helped sheath the *Hambrook*'s sides some years before, also with a mate who had sailed in her and with a creek pilot (known as a 'huffler') who knew quite a lot about her points of sailing.

All this armed me with a useful store of knowledge (for I had never even set foot aboard the *Hambrook* before) and at the same time fortified me with several pints of excellent Kentish ale. Thus emboldened I trudged down the muddy path to the little shipyard on the banks of Milton Creek.

It was very dark when I found the *Hambrook* and she looked a huge massive thing against the night sky and her masts and sails seemed to tower to indefinable heights. But in reality she was a small barge and even in the darkness I could see by her shape aft that she was no flyer. Her uncomely stern was compensated somewhat by a well-shaped bow, and with a boltsprit to give her a finishing touch she looked quite good enough to go to sea with in a 'breeze o' wind', as they say in these parts.

The cabin was spacious and comfortable-looking, especially after I had got a fire going. In the flickering light of my candles I fried my supper and washed it down with a bottle of beer I had brought from the pub. Soon, rolled in my blanket, I was fast asleep on the bare boards of the skipper's bunk.

The next day the mate arrived, bag on shoulder, sea-boots

under arm. He was not a professional seaman but an amateur yachtsman who had until then been a poorly paid clerk in a music publisher's office. Fed up with a mere existence behind a desk, he had for a long time yearned to go to sea, and his yachting experience had given him a faint smattering of seafaring knowledge.

The fact that he had never before set foot aboard a spritsail barge and knew nothing about the rig or the work made me a trifle apprehensive. But mates were hard to get and (the *Hambrook* being a comparatively small barge) I knew that, at a pinch, I could do the greater part of the essential work single handed. So I signed him on and hoped for the best.

The shipwrights were finishing off their jobs aboard and the customary shipyard confusion reigned on deck—shavings everywhere, ropes and wires all over the place, some hatches on and some off, no anchor shackled on, topmast still struck and mizzen sail not bent.

A leeboard was also missing and we were just shipping this when Harry Bottriell, the new mate, stepped aboard. He was obviously feeling a bit lost on a strange deck among all this mess, but I thought it augured well for the future that without waiting to change out of his shore clothes he peeled off his jacket and straightway lent a hand on the leeboard pennant.

That little incident proved to be the keynote of his whole career at sea, for he is now mate in an 8,ooo tons foreign-going steamship. He proved to be a worker from the bottom of his heart. In later days he could never bear to leave a job half or badly done. He never shirked the worst and most soul-searing jobs aboard a sailing barge, and when he eventually left the barges and went into bigger ships he earned the enviable reputation of clean-cut efficiency combined with popularity among the crew. I could never achieve that myself, for I must needs stamp and curse and swear at seamen who are not quick enough or good enough at making sail, sheeting home, making ropes fast properly and suchlike.

Soon the time came to shove off afloat and somehow all the jobs got done by high water. With a fair wind we went sailing down the narrow Milton Creek into the River Swale, thence out into the mouth of the Medway and up Sea Reach to London.

We brought up off Erith to phone for orders, and it turned out that I had to go to the city. Within an hour of my arrival in the broker's office the *Hambrook* was fixed with a full cargo of barley for Colchester. An excellent freight for a start, and right pleased I was when I hurried back to Erith to break the news to Harry. He, in the meantime, had industriously scrubbed the decks, sides and cabin so that the barge was smart and clean for our first cargo.

We were to be alongside a ship in the King George V Dock the next day and when we arrived joined a crowd of other barges waiting on the same ship. Among them were the *Dorothy,* the *Convoy* and the *Beatrice Maud* of our own firm and about a dozen others. And a fine array they made, lying four abreast alongside, their masts and sprits towering high up above the big ship's decks, their ropes in neat Flemish coils and their spars and paintwork glinting in the morning sun. They looked for all the world like rows of racehorses tethered in a stable.

We were one of the last to load and rejoined the outward bound fleet off Southend, where they were lying to their anchors under the lee of the land with a strong wind blowing from the north. Some had been there for several days.

It has been accepted by generations of sailing bargemen that if the wind is 'upalong', as they say, a barge cannot get further than the Southend anchorage unless her skipper is plum crazy. And it is a fact that, even with a moderate breeze blowing from between north and south-east, a loaded barge cannot find any safe anchorage within an ebb tide's sail from Southend. Consequently, if winds persist from this quarter for any length of time a great fleet of loaded sailing barges from up the river accumulates at Southend waiting for a chance to get to the eastward.

When this happens the crews watch each other like hawks in case one should steal a march on the others. If one crew musters and gets under way nearly always someone will follow her, perhaps all the crowd if the weather looks as though the venturesome one might get away and leave them all behind.

You have only to rattle an anchor chain at the crack of dawn to bring heads popping out of cabin scuttles to see what you are up to. I knew one young skipper who used to heave in a few links for devilment and then slack them out again and go and have his breakfast. A few mornings of this nearly caused some of his rivals to have a nervous breakdown, and he was for a time quite a menace to the peace and serenity of the anchorage.

It was in some ways rather unfortunate that on my first trip in the *Hambrook* I also should become a disturber of the peace and forever after was watched with distrust in windbound ports and anchorages by some of the older skippers in case I should give them the slip. Not that I ever wanted to, for it is best that every man should stick to his own judgement and act according to the abilities of his own ship. All I ever did was to get on with the job, and made a rule never to lose a favourable slant of wind. But one or two old wiseacres used to think (and still do) that I was trying to outwit them, whereas such was not the case. I was in barges to make a decent living, not to lie about in smooth water berths and make a comfortable life of it.

What all this led to in one terrible winter's gale I will come to later in my story.

The morning after our sail down to Southend I tumbled out of my bunk before daylight and saw that the wind had shifted a point to the west of north. Satisfied that it was not likely to veer back again I called Harry and we had a quick cup of strong tea.

As the first light streaks of dawn could be seen over the estuary we hove up our anchor, set the topsail and reached out round the pier. I knew that our every move was under observation but we had no time to think about what other people were going to do. There was a smart breeze and a nasty kick in the sea and the topsail, mainsail and foresail were all she wanted, for we had to consider the care of our barley stacked above the coamings. To wet any on our first trip would have been a very bad beginning.

By the time we were sailing down the West Swin channel the tide had run well off the Maplin and Barrow sands on either hand and our whole prospects centred on whether we would be able to fetch through that lonely stretch of water known as South-West Reach. This reach runs in a more northerly direction than the Swin and the tide was due to turn against us before we got through to the Whitaker Spit.

There was too much sea to slam to windward in any case and if we did not get her right through on the port tack there would not be a hope for us against the flood tide.

Soon we saw that we were being followed. Hard astern came the *Gannet* under all plain sail and, further astern still, we could see the outline of other barges coming away from Southend. Before the day was very old a large proportion of the fleet was streaming after us, but we had a long lead and the only one to catch us was the *Gannet*.

We fetched through South-West Reach with only a matter of yards to spare to clear the Middle Ground shoal under our lee. It was here that the *Gannet* overhauled us, gradually working up on our starboard quarter until the wind was more free and she was able to sail through our lee. She made a fine picture as she pranced through the seas, the sunlit spray flying from her bows and the whole ship heeling gracefully and majestically in the harder puffs. The sparkling water was cascading from her scuppers and I could see her old skipper at the wheel nursing her along with all the cunning and skill of a master sailorman.

The tide being in flood, we had enough water to cross over the sands at the Wallet Spitway and go round on the other tack to lay up along the Essex coast to the Knoll buoy. Then came a beat to windward into the River Colne, which leads to Colchester, but every hundred yards we gained towards the land brought us into smoother water.

Now there was one thing that intrigued Harry about spritsail rig—what happened if the sprit came down? Did it ever happen and if so why? Well, I explained as best I could that it did happen and that it could be a catastrophic event.

'Perhaps,' I told him, 'you'll see it happen one day.'

Soon after I had spoken a dark rain-squall descended on us, blotting out everything. Fortunately we had the topsail off her in good time and came to no harm, but the *Gannet,* who had gone on up the River Blackwater, was not so lucky. Just as the rain cleared sufficiently to see a little way I saw her sprit go crashing over the side, ripping the mainsail and topsail to pieces. Harry was busy at the time re-setting our topsail. I called out to him.

'There you are, Harry. The *Gannet's* sprit has gone.'

Harry was sadly disappointed. He hadn't seen it happen.

A few months later we were lying under the lee of the Blyth Sands in Sea Reach with a gale blowing from the south-west when the barge *Scotsman* met with a similar accident just as she was tacking under our stern. Her sprit split clean in half and by the time her skipper could get his helm up and put her before the wind the topsail and mainsail were banging and flogging to leeward in hopeless confusion. Poor Harry didn't see that either as he was down below when it happened.

The third and last occasion when he might have seen a sprit come down was after we had left the *Hambrook* and joined the *Northdown.* He missed seeing that, too, even though it was our own sprit that came down.

To get back to our trip to Colchester. We hustled in to windward and managed to get up the River Colne as far as Fingringhoe, a desolate little place which I knew well from the days when I used to load sand there in the *Audrey.* Here I nipped ashore in the boat and phoned old Bob Eves to come down and tow us up to Colchester with his motor-boat. It is too narrow to sail up to there unless the wind is fair.

Old Bob used to be skipper of the *Terror;* and, with a peaked cap set fairly above a lined and weatherbeaten face which was aptly decorated by a white 'Captain Kettle' beard, he might well have been a character from the books of W. W. Jacobs, or even Captain Kettle himself. The name of his old ship was quite applicable to her skipper.

Bob was well over eighty, but his mate in the motor-boat was a mere seventy-four. Bob referred to him as 'the boy', bemoaning his slowness and sadly prophesying that he would never be any good in a boat. 'The boy', on the other hand, called Bob a 'bloody old so and so' and many were the arguments which flared up between them in the course of taking a barge in tow.

Next day they got us up to the maltings at Colchester and we duly discharged our first cargo, bringing the grand sum of twelve pounds to the crew, that being our half of the freight. Out of this Harry took one third (four pounds) and I took two thirds. The other twelve pounds went into the owner's pocket. That is the share system in almost every barge firm, and it has survived the years as the best and fairest means of distributing the spoils.

We were in luck's way with the weather, for when we were discharged and ready to sail back to London a smart breeze came out of the north-east and away we went.

Soon after Bob Eves had let go our tow rope at Rowhedge we squared off the mainsail and topsail and had the big white staysail set out as a spinnaker as we bowled out past the Bar Buoy at a rattling speed. Since it was only just high water we took a short cut, running over the top of the Buxey Sands in about twelve feet of water, across the mouth of the River Crouch, over the Maplin Sands and out into deep water again off Shoebury.

As we surged up over the ebb we found fifteen of the barges we had left at Southend still lying there windbound.

Our days in the *Hambrook* were happy ones until we fell upon bad times. We had done well with a number of cargoes to Colchester, Sittingbourne, Battlesbridge and Ipswich until work became slack and freights were low. Our earnings dwindled and dwindled and the *Hambrook* used to lie for days and weeks at Woolwich buoys with nothing to do. In the month of June we earned the sum of ten shillings between us. In July we did one cargo to Battlesbridge, bringing our earnings for that month to eleven pounds for the pair of us. I began to look for another ship.

Chapter Six

IT WAS A CUSTOM, almost a ritual, for the skippers of sailing barges to assemble in the back-parlour of the Union Jack tavern at Ipswich during the forenoon, there to discuss the whys and wherefores of coasting in general while the pints flowed freely and the haze of tobacco smoke grew thicker and thicker.

Under the chairmanship of the landlord, an ex-bargeman and steamboat skipper known in almost every port on the East Coast as Sidelight Lucas, the news of the waterside was debated, from the freight rates in London and the alleged roguery of certain brokers to the depth of water at the Stone Banks Buoy or the quality of beer in Yarmouth.

If one wanted to talk about sailing and weather, sets of tides and coasting lore, the Union Jack was the place to go into.

But this particular morning all these things were thrust into the background. There was only one subject—the prospect of war with Germany. Like a black cloud it blotted out all else and subdued the usual hearty and cheerful atmosphere.

The British Premier, Neville Chamberlain, had gone to Germany to negotiate with Hitler, and the fate of Europe, perhaps of the whole world, lay in the balance.

As is generally the case with seafaring men, who do not every day have access to newspapers or listen to arguments and theories in city lunch bars, the gathering at the Union Jack took a very abrupt and honest view of the whole affair. Germany, they all agreed, was out to regain what she had lost in the last war, and if we gave way to her she would eventually pounce on Britain and her Empire. Chamberlain must show Hitler that we weren't afraid of him and stave him off until we had got enough guns and ships and aeroplanes. It was perhaps a pity that at the time more people did not take to the same honest opinion instead of partaking in the hypocritical cant and drivel which was to be heard in public places and read in the newsprint of the day. As to the effect on themselves, most of the older bargemen earnestly hoped that if there was to be war the Naval control of coasting ships would be more sensible than last time. Some hoped it would be more seamanlike, too.

One old fellow recalled how in the last war he had been running his barge before a strong wind through the Edinburgh Channel (which is at the south-eastern part of the Thames Estuary) when a 'la-di-da young officer in a patrol boat' ordered him to 'anchor immediately'. The barge was in deep water with a heavy sea running in from the north-east. The officer insisted on his order being carried out in spite of the protests of the old skipper, and eventually, with the loss of her topsail, the barge was brought to and both anchors let go with sixty fathoms of chain on each. Three days passed before the crew were able to get them up again, by which time the patrol officer had 'disappeared and forgotten us.'

At the time I was inclined to take this and similar tales with a pinch of salt, but in due course I was to find ample confirmation from my own experiences.

At this critical time I was in the process of changing ships. Harry and I were discharging our last cargo from the *Hambrook.* We were to take over the famous racing barge *Northdown* at Sittingbourne, where she had just completed a re-fit.

The *Northdown* lay on the blocks in an evil smelling gutway off Milton Creek. It was not exactly a cheerful spot to begin life on a new ship, for the place was overrun with rats and the stench of the creek quite sickening.

We were glad to get away from it and breathe a little decent air when we sailed beyond King's Ferry on the way to London for orders. But, alas! It was only to find that coasting work was slack and we were to load coal back to Milton. There were several cargoes of this coal from Poplar Dock and there was nothing for it but to fill in the time in this way and earn a few pounds until the corn market brightened up again.

Harry and I were neither hopeful nor encouraged during our first few weeks aboard the *Northdown,* although we had the compensation of finding her a wonderfully fast and handy ship. All we did was trade between the smoke and dust of London and the stink and slime of Milton Creek.

It was an awful spot to trade to. Even the people there were most depressing and formed one of the black spots in English life.

Sometimes our coal was hove out by grab and crane on the banks of the creek where some land was being reclaimed. To this

place hundreds of tons of London garbage were brought in old
lighters and dirty barges and dumped there with waste ashes and
clinker. The whole area was one vast rubbish heap bordered by
the evil smelling waters of the tortuous creek.

Over this ghastly waste there roamed in the evenings human
beings who themselves looked so dirty, pallid and poverty-
stricken that they seemed almost akin to the beady-eyed rats who
scampered brazenly about their feet. These people were so poor
that they picked over the garbage in search of anything which
might be of use.

They would find a rusty old kitchen knife, a battered
saucepan, discarded items of clothing and miscellaneous articles
mixed in with the muck which I would not have touched with a
ten-foot boom. Like starving vultures they pecked and scraped
for these treasured things quite unconscious of the stink, the rats
and the dreadful humiliation of such an occupation.

I talked to some of these scarecrows—tried to find out what
they knew or thought of the world's great happenings such as the
Munich crisis (which was then at its height) and whether they
realised that the fate of millions was at that time in the balance.
But so lowly were they and possibly undernourished that their
minds seemed numb to it all and the best to be extracted from
their thoughts was that wars and politics were arranged for the
benefit of a rich few.

They were quite resigned to whatever might befall them.
After all, what had these poor souls to lose, no matter whether
the days to come were doomed to the wracks of war or the so-
called blessings of peace? The effects of either would be blunted
upon their desperate existence.

The prospect of air raids and bombing did not stir them in the
least, and the whole idea of another world-war was regarded only
with a strange but philosophical misunderstanding.

It was the sight of these haggard crows on the banks of Milton
Creek that made me resolve never to let poverty overtake me to
such an extent that I might fall with them into their pit of
hopelessness and helplessness.

All this squalor and filth was a part of Kent: the Garden of
England as it is called. It seemed almost unbelievable. Even after
all these years I sometimes think I can still smell the place. And I

think of it too when I hear the yards and yards of flapdoodle poured out by well-meaning theorists and politicians who are trying to plan and promise a wonderful new world for ordinary men.

It might well be said that a bargeman lives on the fringe of the world, almost in a world of his own, from which he can observe lives and doings of all manner of people. While I have been in the barges I have had a full view of what poverty, distress and ignorance can do to people who would otherwise be honest, healthy and intelligent.

I have worked among them, been into their musty homes (often bug-ridden), talked and tippled with them, and have seen the core of staunch folk rotting under the burdens of overwork and undernourishment. Worse still is the effect on their children, for whom there is no money to buy milk, no money to provide proper and regular meals, no money to buy warm clothes for the winter, no money to give them a good education, no time for the overworked parents even to keep them clean.

I am no social reformer. I have neither the brains nor the vision nor the ability. But I have always said that one day I would set down in print my impressions of that heap of garbage and human relics on the banks of Milton Creek. And now that I have done it I will go back to my story.

We had little to grumble about as far as the *Northdown* was concerned. I have never sailed in a faster vessel or in one which would always appear so ready to do the impossible. Sailing barges often get into awkward positions when going in and out of docks, sailing to and from wharves, or getting under way from crowded anchorages. But the *Northdown* would always do that little bit extra, even under the most scanty canvas, that would save us heaving her out to windward or perhaps waiting for a turn of the tide. For her size, 195 tons to her marks, I would be so bold as to say that she was the fastest and handiest barge hull ever built. She was weakly constructed and she often strained and whipped and leaked; but that did not detract from her sailing qualities. Especially was she a joy to me at the wheel, for I had been brought up in lumbering old schooners and the slower and more cumbersome types of barges. I began to think she was almost a witch and would do anything for me.

When our cargoes of coal to Milton Creek were finished I was able to fix her with 150 tons of oil cake to Great Yarmouth. We loaded it out of a Greek ship in the Millwall dock and with an ideal westerly breeze bowled off down the river and anchored for the flood tide inside the Yantlet Buoy in Sea Reach.

Before daylight the next morning we were off again under mainsail, foresail and topsail and soon afterwards set the big white staysail on the short topmast stay. Under this canvas, with the wind edging on the port quarter, she ran like a hare and steered as easily as a lifeboat.

All was going so well that I could not envisage any sort of trouble, only a swift and pleasant passage, even though it was November. But off Shoebury it became necessary to give her a bit more mainsheet and slack away the weather vang. As I did so there was a creaking, cracking noise aloft and for a moment I could not think what it was. The mate was unhooking the lee backstay when there came a sudden crash accompanied by the sound of splintering timber.

The sprit had broken; and as it crashed over the side the huge spar narrowly missed the head of the unsuspecting Harry.

'Christ,' he yelled, 'what's happened?'

'The sprit's fallen down,' I said.

Harry paused for a moment and then looked at me with a wry smile.

'There,' he said, 'and I didn't even see it happen.'

So Harry never did fulfil his curiosity of seeing a barge's sprit come down, even when it was our own that broke.

We were in a fine pickle. The spar had broken about half-way up, and the mainsail, vangs, and other gear were trailing in a frightful tangle over the lee quarter. It was ebb tide and a smart westerly breeze, so that there was no turning back just then; it flashed through my mind that perhaps I could get to Yarmouth under jury rig. So Harry took the wheel while I sorted out all the bits and pieces and found to my relief that the mainsail had not been torn.

By the time we reached the Spitway most of the gear had been hauled aboard and cleared up and we thereupon anchored to wait for water over the sands. Meantime we began to work out our jury rig, for it was better to get to Yarmouth and get the cargo out than summon a tow back to London or Sittingbourne. Our oil-cake was stacked up well above the coamings, and re-rigging the barge without shifting it was going to be a heap of trouble.

We put Irishman's reefs (big knots) in the clew and tack of the topsail so that it would set, after a fashion, between the topmast and the broken end of the sprit, just above the yard-tackle. Then we rigged vangs on the remains of the sprit and fetched out a huge boltsprit jib which had been used for racing. This we set as a trysail abaft the mainmast, hooking the head on to the mainhorse traveller.

When the tide flowed over the Spitway we were under way again and doing a good four knots with a moderate southwest wind. As we ran past Harwich the wind veered to west and the big staysail began to do more work, so that by nightfall we were off Aldeburgh. She must have looked a strange sight from the shore.

Fortunately the weather was all in our favour, but going in to the land through the Stanford Channel off Lowestoft we were well pleased to find that she would even stand close-hauled on the wind.

Sailing vessels have to tow into Yarmouth harbour when the wind is off the land, and as we approached the pier-heads the paddle tug *United Services—67* years old—came out to meet us.

The skipper of the tug contended that we were a casualty and wanted to tow us in as salvage; but that wasn't going to come off after we had sailed her some eighty miles under jury rig. I demanded ordinary towage rates.

So we bluffed and swore at each other, although we were really quite good friends and had had many a pint together in the Cellar House when I had been mate of the *Oceanic*.

Dusk was falling and still we could not agree, and at the end of a lot of shouting and argument the tug returned to harbour and left us to our fate. I knew he would come back in the morning in case the wind should shift and we might get the barge in without his help. It would look bad for the tugmaster if he refused double-towage and then lost the job altogether.

So all that night we pitched and rolled at our anchor and the wind held westerly and fine, straight off the land. In the morning it was still the same and there was hardly any hope of getting into the harbour under our jury sails. Yarmouth is the worst harbour on the east coast to enter. The northern pier-head is of wooden piles so that the flood tide, which runs very strongly, can boil through it. The other pier is shorter and of stone so that the tide water hits it and creates a sort of whirlpool right in the entrance. There is also a right-angled bend just inside so that the only favourable wind to sail a ship in with is south-east, and that kicks up a short breaking sea on the bar.

I will not bore the uninitiated with the various other difficulties a sailor has to face in taking this harbour, for they are very involved and numerous, but those I have mentioned are the more important.

Sure enough the tug came steaming out again at seven o'clock and within a few minutes we had come to terms and the tow-rope was on the hook. Even under tow it takes two men to steer a big barge through that entrance on the flood; but once round the corner we rapidly passed up the harbour between the long quays which accommodate all manner of ships and boats—anything from diminutive shrimpers to trawlers, barges and the big Baltic timber ships.

As we went by Jewson's wharf we saw a number of barges lying windbound and all the skippers and crews gathered on the quay to see the 'casualty' come in, for no doubt they had heard all about us from the tugmaster the night before. They looked rather astonished when, in reply to their questions, we sang out that we had lost our sprit at the Mouse. No one had ever sailed a barge that far without a sprit before.

We berthed in the North River, as coasting men call the mouth of the Bure, and being discharged a couple of days later towed down to Fellowes shipyard to get a new sprit. It was specially made for us, being a splendid piece of pine sixty-seven feet long. A young shipwright shaped it out single-handed in four days and made a beautiful job of it. He was a trained craftsman who had served a long and diligent apprenticeship to his trade, a type of worker which is becoming all too scarce in these times.

We lowered our mast down and got the new sprit shipped. Other bargemen turned to with a will and lent us a hand. They had been held up for a long time by strong southerly and westerly winds, some of them as long as ten weeks, during which time many had practically spent out and were getting very hard up. That is the snag about cargoes to Yarmouth. Unless the wind shifts for the return trip the round voyage is apt to take so long that the profits have disappeared before the barge gets back to London.

When at last we were all ready for sea the wind was blowing half a gale from the south-west and we had to bide our time like the others. For three days it blew hard and the skippers passed the time playing darts for beer in the Anson Arms, under the auspices of that grand old host, Ike. He was a good friend to bargemen and was soon to prove it after the adventures which were to befall us.

Chapter Seven

ONE MORNING THE SKY BECAME more sullen and grey and the clouds travelled less swiftly along the coast from the southward. There was a little rain and a few bright patches of blue sky over the low hills to the west of the harbour. There was hope of a change in the weather.

There was much pacing of decks and consultations in one another's cabins, but until Ike had opened the doors of the Anson the wind still persisted from the south-west, though by no means as strongly as during the last few days. I noticed that while the ensuing games of darts were in progress the skipper of the *Una*, Harry Filmer, who ranked with the best and most skilful of bargemen, frequently walked to the window and glanced up at the ever-brightening sky. I knew that he was itching to go but did not want to tow away to sea and leave some of his old friends in harbour who did not think the weather fit to start. It was the more elderly masters who had no faith in any improvement in the weather and deprecated any idea that we might muster in the afternoon. To their sorrow they did not stick to their opinions. It was November and the barometer was still low.

By the time we strolled back along the quay to have dinner the wind had shifted well to the west and I told Filmer that I was going to order the tug. He said that if I was going to sea he would come too. So away he went after his stores while I got on the phone to the Harbour Master for a tow out of the harbour. It was three o'clock and we should have all the flood tide to help us make Harwich in the morning should the weather become bad again. The *Northdown* was a fast barge and the mate and I were both young, strong and active. I felt convinced that we should get round Orfordness before the wind backed, and reach smoother water before having the punch to windward.

Within a short time the old paddle tug ranged alongside.

'Anyone else a-coming,' shouted the tugmaster.

'Yes,' I replied, 'the *Una* will. She's lying with the others down at Jewson's.'

As we came abreast of the other barges and slowed down the skipper of the *Una* waved us away and shook his head. He had changed his mind and was not coming. The other crews sat on their hatches and watched us swinging out the boat, rather uncertain, so it turned out later, whether to call us bloody fools or come with us. But they all stayed put and off we went alone.

It was half past three in the afternoon when we cast off our tow-rope and the tide was sluicing up through the roads so that by the time we had set the mainsail, topsail and foresail and got everything in nice trim we were abreast of Lowestoft. Close-hauled on the starboard tack, we could just fetch our course along the land, sagging off only a little with our own leeway. There was only a moderate sea and the barge rolled and surged along in fine style, thumping occasionally as barges will on a steep sided white-cap and sending the spume flying across the fore hatches.

As we passed the lighthouse which stands in the middle of the town at Southwold we were about five miles off the land and the wind began to head us a little and freshen. This meant that to make our passage we must not give way an inch to leeward during the next fifteen miles to Orfordness. But, as is so often the case in these parts, the further south we sailed the more southerly became the wind, and by the time the flashes of the Ness light were on our beam the ebb tide was away and we were being driven far to the eastward.

Rain came; and then a heavy squall, so heavy that we dare not put the vessel about on the other tack for fear of losing all our canvas if it shook. With each high screech of the wind in the rigging it edged more and more to the southward. Squalls came quickly one after the other and within a couple of hours a raging gale was at its height. I felt thankful that the rotten old sprit had broken in fine weather and not hung up there long enough to let us down on such a night as this.

Harry had let the head of the topsail run down with the first squall and under main and fore the *Northdown* was making good weather of it all, in spite of the heavy seas which were by then piling up on her weather bow and knocking her head to leeward. I began to think out a plan of action in case of emergency.

Were we to stand on our course at the time we should eventually arrive off the Flemish banks in the neighbourhood of Zeebrugge, which would be a weather shore and fit to anchor under the lee of until the weather moderated. I knew that stretch of coast fairly well and was by no means dismayed at the thought of a trip to the Continent, however unforeseen it might be.

A better prospect was to get her round on to the port tack in a smooth patch so that she would fetch into Harwich as the flood tide came in the small hours before daybreak.

The third and most desperate idea was that if by cruel chance we should lose our sails or spars the helm should be put up and the barge run before the wind until we were round the Cockle to the north of Yarmouth, where the land curves westward and the wind would be at a sufficient angle off the land to ensure smoother water and a fairly safe anchorage.

Little did Harry and I suspect that all the other barges from Yarmouth had put to sea as well, the skippers having all changed their minds when the tug returned from towing the *Northdown* out. Far astern of us they were all in fearful straits, battling against terrible seas on a lee shore, their sails blown away and some with masts and spars gone as well. Several were sinking or half full of water, so that their exhausted crews were glad to be rescued by the gallant efforts of the local lifeboatmen from Aldeburgh and Yarmouth.

We had the advantage of having started with the first flush of tide, and were thus far enough to the southward to escape the worst of their predicament, for when the ebb tide came away none of them had reached the Ness. It was between Yarmouth Roads and Orfordness that the full weight of the gale and the heaviest seas were to be experienced.

Our own troubles were bad enough in all conscience.

Once I tried to put the barge about in a smoothish patch, but a steep sea hit her on the weather bow just as she was almost up into the wind, and for one awful moment the sails gave a violent shake before she fell away on to the same tack again.

Every stitch had held.

About half an hour later I tried her again, and to our great relief the sails came over. Harry hung on to the rigging to let go the bowline as she bore away on the new tack. He dare not let the foresail bang across the horse with the full weight of the wind in it, for it might have kept going; so, in spite of a considerable amount of salt water inside his shirt, he had to stick it until he could gradually ease the bowline inch by inch.

Harry made the bowline fast when the foresail was halfway

over, and thus we let the barge lie partly hove to, although she was still racing through the water at a speed sufficient to make her pound and plunge into the white-capped seas. With the foresail half aback I was able to ease the wheel and the strain was thereby taken off the steering gear.

The starboard leeboard had been lowered half-way to prevent her from being blown to leeward too rapidly and, although we had often done some swearing about the great size and weight of the *Northdown's* leeboards (especially on occasions when we had to heave them up quickly), I was thankful for their stoutness on this memorable morn. A light or even medium leeboard would have broken under the leeward drift of the barge in such weather. She would have been then like a lame duck and we might have found ourselves in a perilous situation, to say the least of it.

But as things were, with the spars, sails and rigging all standing the strain, and the half-leeboard doing its work, I knew that, bar accidents, all would be well with us.

For six hours we let her lie to her bowline, the spray flying over us and drenching our cold tired bodies again and again. I eased her through the seas as best I could, but now and then she would make my stomach sink as her flat bottom reared up and banged down, making her shudder from stem to stern. I have a vivid recollection of the mate hanging on to the mizzen rigging and performing a miracle by getting his pipe alight, only to have the wad of glowing tobacco blown clean out of the bowl and away into the gloom like a tiny rocket.

Break of day gave us our first glimpse of the scene about us and of the power of the elements which we had hitherto fought only in darkness. It was one of those mornings which almost every seaman has seen at some time or other in some part of the world, once or twice if he be lucky or many a time if he has lived to become old and wise in companionship with the sea.

Each of the short, steep seas was white topped and its back streaked with foam by the force of the wind. And each hollow was blotted out by a driving, misty spume. In the midst of it all our little wooden world of eighty-nine feet plunged and wallowed as she battled for our lives—and we for hers.

Over us the low clouds careered helter skelter from the southward, reducing even broad daylight to a kind of hazy dusk. The land could not be seen, but about nine o'clock we saw the

S.W. Bawdsey buoy lurching drunkenly on our weather beam. I knew then that we were to windward of Harwich Harbour, a fine broad refuge, easy to enter and affording ample shelter in either of the two rivers which empty into it.

Now was the time to take even greater care, for a wrong turn of the wheel or bad trimming of the main sheet and vangs could yet land us in disaster. The foresail was let draw and I brought the vessel well off the wind, for I knew the way into Harwich Harbour blindfold, so many times had I sailed in and out of there.

But just as she bore up the gale, vicious enough in all conscience, seemed to reach a crescendo of violence and screeched through the rigging like a thousand devils. I yelled to Harry to help me with the wheel and together we kept her away and dare not touch a vang or a sheet, for they were both bar taut and might have broken with the surge had we tried to ease them.

The speed of the barge was terrific, even with the main sheet hard in, and thus we had to let her rip and steer a wild course towards the land.

If only we could have brailed the sail up to the sprit so that the barge would run comfortably before the wind I should have been both happy and confident. But with the full mainsail still set and sheeted home I knew that there were several dangers which might beset us, too technical to describe in detail here but principally concerned with the carrying away of essential hooks and shackles, or the possible failure of the steering gear to withstand the strain. Not the least was the fact that the vessel would not bear up; and indeed this nearly brought about our downfall with safety close at hand.

We caught a fleeting glimpse of the Cork Lightship which is moored off Felixstowe to the east of the harbour entrance, and the *Northdown* shot between the fairway buoys like a mad thing, covered with spray and foam. Then we had to make a right-angled turn to run into the harbour, but the pressure on the wheel was so great that two of us could hardly turn it. Harry on the lee side had both hands and feet on the spokes, striving to pull them down towards him, while I pressed upward with all the strength I could muster.

The wind did not ease even for a second to allow us to get her heading into the harbour, and all she did was race across the deep water channel and make a beeline for the stone breakwater and shoals on the other side. She did bear up a trifle and we only missed hitting the Cliffe Foot buoy by a hair's-breadth.

I decided on a last desperate measure. That mainsail had to be got off her or else we should be smashed up and drowned at the very gate of our sanctuary. I screwed down the steering brake which locked the wheel, and went to the mainsheet. Harry scrambled forward to the brail winch. I started to ease away the sheet. Harry hove like a Titan on the winch handle. Inch by inch the wire brail took up the after cloths of the great sail and as the pressure eased her head slowly turned harbourwards. All was well. I quickly made the sheet fast and got back to the wheel. Harry came aft and once more took hold of the lee spokes. With barely a hundred yards to spare from the breakwater, over which the seas were flying in an awe-inspiring manner, the *Northdown* bore away before the wind and darted into the sheltered waters of Harwich.

Within a very short time the sails were stowed up and the anchor was down with thirty-five fathoms of chain to hold her. We thought that we might afford the luxury of a rest, a smoke and a cup of tea, but the weather seemed to get worse and worse, so that conditions, even in the harbour, became dangerous.

Another barge near us, named the *Blue Mermaid*, started walking away with her anchor as though it wasn't there. A squall took her right across the harbour broadside to the wind and she just missed a seaplane moored off the Felixstowe side. Her crew managed to get her mizzen sail set so that she came up head to wind and, with plenty of scope of chain, her anchor bit again, holding her only a few yards off the sea wall. Eventually the crew scrambled some sail on her, got the anchor up, and sailed her to a safer berth—all of which was no mean feat of seamanship.

We in our turn dragged across the steamship fairway, giving her chain all the time, until she brought herself up in the deep water with fifty fathoms of cable bar-taut out ahead of her. The strain on the chain was so great that the links bit through the wooden sheathing on the windlass barrel.

There we lay all that day and all the next night, keeping anchor watches and fearing all the time that the express steam packet boats from Denmark and Holland would cut us down in the darkness. Not until dawn did the gale abate and we started on the arduous job of heaving in all that heavy chain so that we could shift out of the fairway to a comfortable anchorage. It struck me at the time that a bargeman's life is a very hard one.

•••••

While grappling with our own difficulties I had not for one moment thought that any of the barges in Yarmouth had come out and been caught in the gale. In fact I did not learn the story of their various misfortunes until about a week later. And a harrowing tale it all made.

Apparently some of the skippers changed their minds for a second time after the tug had taken the *Northdown* out of the harbour. It would look bad for them, they thought, to remain in harbour, especially after lying windbound for so many weeks, while the *Northdown* stole a passage back to London. So in the end, some still dubious about the weather and others mustering partly against their will, they all decided to go scrambling after the *Northdown.*

But the day was getting old; and before the last of them was out of the harbour darkness had fallen and the tide was well spent. What was more, many of these barges were slow or not built for bad weather coasting work. There is no doubt that it was the fatal folly of indecision which eventually threw them all to the mercy of that terrible gale. The *Northdown,* a fast barge and built to ride a heavy sea, was half-way to Harwich before any of these followers had got as far as Lowestoft.

It was the following morning that people in Yarmouth heard the lifeboat crew being called out, and soon small crowds collected on the pier and along the cliffs at Gorleston.

The barges were running back under bare poles, some with their masts and sprits gone overboard, some half-full of water and others desperately trying to hold their vessels head-to-sea with two anchors.

Old Ike, mine host of the Anson Arms, was there to watch the crews he had served with pints of beer the day before struggling for their lives in the midst of the white-capped fury of the North Sea.

The *Una* and the *Decima* came flying from the southward, the *Una* apparently unharmed, but the *Decima* steering wildly with her sails blown to pieces and streaming in tatters from the spars and rigging.

Harry Filmer, the master of the *Una,* took what was undoubtedly the wisest course in the circumstances. With his son Tom, who was mate, helping him at the wheel, he steered the *Una* head first through the breakers for the beach and slammed her hard ashore just to leeward of the Wellington pleasure pier. The lifeboat immediately began to manoeuvre as near to her as possible to get the crew off in case they were washed overboard, but the stout-hearted Harry waved them away and pointed to the *Decima*.

Her skipper, the tall and genial Fred Walker, had not been so fortunate and was in the greater need of help. She had been driven straight for the offshore Scroby sands, over which huge seas were thundering, and the anchor was let go in a hopeless attempt to bring her head to sea and to hold her away from what seemed inevitable destruction until the lifeboat could take off the crew. She struck just as the lifeboat reached her and the skipper and mate, a youngster named Joe Monk, made a flying leap to comparative safety. As the *Decima*'s rudder hit the sand her head reared up, spun round athwart the seas and fell with a crash on the iron-hard sand. Then up came her stern in a wild sweep to strike again higher up on the shoal. Thus, first one end and then the other, she was hurled in a mad career through the breakers and right across the Scroby into the deep water to the eastward. The last the watchers at Yarmouth saw of her she was still afloat and being driven rapidly to the north-east.

About a week later the derelict was washed up on the coast of Holland, eventually to be salvaged and brought back to her owners at Grays in Essex. As I write these lines, several years later, she lies under the stern of my barge off Yantlet Creek waiting for the ebb tide to take her down-swin with a cargo of linseed for Ipswich. No one would have thought she would ever be seen again on that memorable day when Fred Walker and Joe Monk jumped for their lives as she hit the Scroby.

Two other barges, the *Grecian* and the *Astrild,* were driven across the North Sea on to the Dutch coast. Their crews had been taken off by the Aldeburgh lifeboat several miles out from the Suffolk coast after they had lost all sails, spars and anchors. Poor old George Mead, the master of the *Grecian* and one of the finest bargemen on the east coast, was almost heartbroken at the loss of his ship, for she sank among the Dutch shoals and could not be recovered. But the *Astrild* was eventually salvaged and was towed home with the *Decima*.

The hardest luck of all came to young Dick King, the skipper of the old wooden barge *Cetus*. He had been at anchor off Southwold when the wind freshened to a gale and had succeeded in getting his anchor and running his barge off before the wind, which at that time was slightly to the east of south. Dick immediately resolved to try and run into Lowestoft, for it is an easier harbour to enter than Yarmouth, and can be made in a sailing vessel with a south-east gale provided she can be steered reasonably well and the helmsman exercises a very exact judgement.

The *Cetus* ran close to the shore by Pakefield and was approaching the southern arm of the harbour when a big salvage tug, no doubt sensing good business to be done, came plunging out right across the barge's head. No one was at fault, for neither vessel was in sight of the other until they were almost in collision, the high solid pier-head blocking each skipper's view.

The *Cetus* was tearing through the water at a great speed and had she hit the tug would have probably bashed her stem in and sunk there and then with little chance of her crew being saved from the breakers. They would have been dashed to pieces in a few seconds on the sea wall.

So poor Dick had to bear up to miss the tug, and, it being ebb tide, missed the harbour as well. I could never quite get out of Dick what he called the tug; but he had been brought up in sailing barges from his schoolboy days and no doubt knew how to give vent to his feelings.

Away went the barge to the northward, her crew helpless and faced with the prospect of being blown right away from England to founder in the lonely wastes of the cold North Sea. She was leaking and her rudder was damaged by a heavy sea. So the lifeboat, whose crew was having a busy time, took Dick and the mate out of the barge off Caister.

The *Cetus,* half-full of water, was eventually blown ashore in Germany but later salvaged. Like the *Decima,* she is also in commission to this day. She was refitted at Grays and made into a better barge than she had been before her trip to Germany.

The *Royalty* was fortunate enough to get a tug to tow her into Yarmouth harbour. She had lost all her sails and broken the sprit but otherwise had not come to any great harm. The *Raybel,* too, was lucky, for she let go her anchors in the roads and hung on for several hours. Then the fluke broke off the main anchor and the tug, which was standing by, got a rope aboard her and towed her into Yarmouth. All she lost were her anchors and sails.

Into the middle of all this sea of trouble came a loaded barge
which had been plodding up from the Humber with coal for
Margate Gas Works. She was the *Britisher,* belonging to
Greenhithe, and her skipper was a wily old sea-dog by the name
of George Quinton. His troubles started with the mainsail being
blown away, but he managed to get the barge under the lee of the
Scroby in Yarmouth Roads and let go his main anchor with as
much chain as he had in the locker. For several hours she lay
there, sometimes dragging a little way and sometimes holding.
But when the wind started to veer from south-south-east to south-
west, George found himself almost touching the edge of the
Scroby, the change of wind having converted the sands from a
partial protection to a positive danger. Soon the seas were
sweeping over the barge and George and his mate hung on to the
mizzen rigging fearing that she would break open and sink or that
they would be washed overboard.

The hard-working lifeboat came and took them off, but
George maintained that the barge could be saved and asked for
some of the hands in the lifeboat to go back aboard with him.

The crews of the other barges having by this time been put
safely ashore, the lifeboatmen went back to the *Britisher.* The tug
United Services came and stood by while they hove up the
anchor and helped George to set what was left of the topsail. A
tow rope was passed to the tug and with the topsail helping the
barge to windward she was brought to the harbour entrance. Here
she became almost unmanageable in the heavy seas on the bar
and everything depended on whether the tow-rope would hold.
The tug, which was old and not overburdened with power, got
between the pier-heads, but the *Britisher* charged straight for
Gorleston Pier on the top of a white curling sea. The crowd
turned and ran as the barge's boltsprit swept over the pier and
Quinton, hanging on to the forestay with a chopper in his hand,
was about to cut the towrope at the stem head as it looked as
though the tug was going one side of the pier and the barge the
other. He knew that if the barge was not going into the harbour it
would be best for her to blow ashore on the sandy shelf close to
it, from which he and his helpers might scramble to safety.

Just as she reached the pier another sea hit her just by the
fore-horse and she gave a violent lurch which caused her literally

to fall into the harbour—and into safety.

There was one more barge out in this gale, the old *Martha,* in charge of the elderly Frank Day and his son Albert. Those two were a fine crew, for the old man had been in sail all his life and had passed on his splendid knowledge of seamanship to the boy, who has since become a worthy successor to his tough old dad.

They let go their main anchor in Corton Roads, a mile or two south of Yarmouth harbour, and paid out a generous scope of chain. They lashed everything down, put a tight stow on all their canvas, and rode out the storm without dragging an inch. When the gale blew itself out they set sail again and made Harwich harbour six days later.

Frank Day had often said before that he put great faith in the holding power of that anchor, and this was indeed proof of his words.

Chapter Eight

BAD LUCK SEEMED to dog us with a wretched persistence. Twice we put out of Harwich harbour only to be bowled back again by heavy squalls and south-westerly gales.

On the second occasion a great fleet of us, some thirty barges all told, made a brave start at daybreak, all bound for London. Many a rent and hasty patch could be seen among the cluster of red sails to tell a silent story of the heavy weather of the past week. It looked as though we should all get up to London River at last, for the breeze had petered out in the night and veered round to the north-west.

That is generally a good sign.

We in the *Northdown* were one of the last to get under way, and by the time we reached the Naze the leading barges were half-way up the Wallet—about off Frinton. Then a wicked black cloud swelled up from the south-west. Our north-west breeze died away to a calm. For nearly half an hour all the barges lay still upon the water, slowly driving westwards on the flood tide, their sails hanging in lifeless creases, the loaded ones gently slopping the water into their scuppers with the gentle swell.

Then it hit us—a southerly squall. We could see the white on the water a mile away. Most of the bargemen, though still becalmed, dropped their topsails down or else hove on their main brails, so that the squall should not catch them with too much canvas set. They could always set it again if it were to turn out not so bad as it looked.

It was as bad as we wanted anyway. As the wind came upon us with vicious suddenness, we all up-helm and got our vessels before the wind, racing away to the north-east like a herd of frightened deer. Within a couple of hours we were all anchored once more in Harwich harbour.

This little episode was sufficient to prove to Harry and me that the *Northdown,* although empty, was making a considerable amount of water, for as she surged through the little short seas off the Naze on our way back to Harwich we could hear the water sloshing about down below. Back in harbour we took off some hatches and descended into the main hold to investigate. There was water on the floor of the hold, not much, but enough to cause misgivings. Obviously the gale we had survived coming up from Yarmouth had done her more harm than I thought.

We pumped her out and she was no more trouble while at anchor in smooth water; but when eventually we did get on our way to London in fine weather she leaked so abominably that I had to sail her 'up the Whitaker' (as bargemen call the entrance to the River Crouch) to a smooth water anchorage near the South-West Buxey buoy. It was as well I did so because the bad weather came kicking back at us again that night and it blew great guns from the south-south-west. We did not mind because we were in sheltered water, especially on the ebb, but some of the other barges who had gone on up the Swin had a pretty hectic night.

Daylight showed us the Whitstable barge *Lord Churchill* perched high up on the Foulness Sands, whither she had been forced to run for safety in the darkness. Her skipper told me afterwards that had the tide not fallen so sharply (owing to the southerly wind) the *Churchill* would have gone right over the top of the sands and into the deeper water where we were sheltering. But his action was a safe one, nevertheless, for it is one advantage of a barge's flat bottom that in bad weather it is possible to run her on to a shelving shore. By the time she is aground, being of light draft, there is not enough depth of water to kick up any sea that would harm her seriously. Of course, considerable experience and local knowledge are required before being able to take such a course, but similar action has saved many a barge and her crew in the estuary of the Thames.

Our leak in the *Northdown* persisted, and in the end I put her ashore on a mud flat near Burnham. Here we made the remarkable discovery that the pump pipe on the port side forward had been forced downwards into the bottom planks of the barge, pushing one of them down far enough to cause a rupture and let in a considerable amount of water. This must have happened when she was pounding in those heavy seas off Orfordness. As her flat head thumped down, she being of a build that was far from rigid, the whole hull had worked and whipped so that the iron pump had gone down through her bottom. When we had used that particular pump (there were four all told) we had been pumping the North Sea straight up through the barge and out of the scuppers.

This meant putting her on the nearest blocks, which were at Paglesham and belonged to a well-known local boat builder named Frank Shuttlewood. His father before him had built barges as well as boats, and Frank was very interested in the way the *Northdown* was constructed, for he had heard much of her fame as a racing barge. I am afraid he was a trifle disappointed. Her build was not of the best and stoutest, in spite of her graceful shape, speed, and wonderful handiness in manoeuvre.

He said that he had heard only once before of such a thing happening to a barge. Years ago his father had spoken of a Wakering barge pounding her forward pumps down through her bottom in a Christmas gale off Harwich. But no one else I ever asked had heard of such a thing.

We could not stay long at Paglesham and I was sorry. The place has a quiet, pretty remoteness from the rest of the world and breathes a peace which is typical of these Essex creeks. Paglesham has but a small and exclusive circle of admirers. A few yachtsmen know it, some oyster fishermen know it and local bargemen know it. But the rest of the world will probably never find out where it is or even learn that it exists at all. Which is just as well.

So from the sweet peace of Paglesham we sailed back to the stink and slime of Milton Creek and Sittingbourne where, on our owners' own repair yard, we got the *Northdown* into fighting trim again.

Our misfortunes in getting to and from Yarmouth—the gale, the broken sprit and the leak—had resulted in our taking a month to complete the round trip. But in the end we profited thereby, for a London broker offered me a series of cargoes of oil cake to Yarmouth, work which eventually lasted us the whole winter. This was partly because some owners were a bit dubious about sending their barges to Yarmouth after the disasters of the November gale. Some of the skippers were a bit dubious too; not for the same reason as the owners but because freights were low and there was not much reward in the work if the bad weather kept them windbound in harbours for weeks at a time.

It was a rough winter. Gale after gale, mostly from the south and south-west, lashed the East Coast and more than one barge was lost and her crew drowned in those black, stormy nights.

Through it all we earned a reasonably good living. We hid ourselves away in sheltered anchorages during the gales (generally within reach of some comfortable inn or tavern) and, not without anxiety, stole our passages during the fine spells.

One day we laid alongside the *Oceanic* in Yarmouth. She was a two hundred and fifty tons iron barge in which I had once served as mate. George Eastland, the skipper, was a Littlehampton man who had been reared in the old boom-rigged vessels on the south coast. During my service with him I had learned to respect his seamanship, enterprise and determination. On his part, he always looked upon me as a potential rival to his own fame as a hustler.

There we were, side by side, both bound to London light, and each ready to raise the very devil to be the first barge to drop anchor in the Thames. Of course, it was not the thing even to mention the word 'race' or appear to be in any sort of hurry to round the Ness. We would go ashore together, casually discuss the weather over a pint of beer, and suggest indifferently that 'we *might* jog away up if the wind frees out'. For either to give the slightest hint that he would drive his vessel to the very limit of safety, and beyond, in order to beat the other would have been a gross breach of the most elementary etiquette among sailing skippers.

The *Oceanic* had one great quality when she was light. She would run like a hare before the wind, even though she was a very devil to steer. On any other point of sailing she was no great shakes, but with a fair wind she would take some beating, even by a barge like the *Northdown.* Our main advantage lay in working to windward, and there was not likely to be much of that.

Each morning Eastland and I paced up and down the quarters, eyeing each other warily and watching for a break in the clouds to the southward or any sign of rain. Then, on this particular morning, the wind flew into the north-west just after daylight and I hurried ashore to phone for the tug to take us out to sea.

The noise of our topsail sheet block brought Eastland tumbling out on deck, and when he learned that I had ordered the tug he began to get ready to come too.

With sheets out and main blocks hooked, the crews of both barges stumped up and down the decks impatiently.

The tug had never been noted for its punctuality and it was ten o'clock before she started to tow us down the harbour. None of the other barges attempted to muster, probably because the wind was still blowing with great force. The November gale was yet fresh in the memory.

Among these other vessels was the *Celtic,* sister ship to the *Oceanic,* and Eastland was naturally anxious to be back in London before her. But he had little to worry about on that account because old Jimmy Burrell, the skipper of the *Celtic,* was at that very time expressing the opinion to several other masters congregated on his deck that the weather was not fit for a dog to be out in. They were all moored up some way away from the *Northdown* and *Oceanic* and did not know that we had ordered the tug. Even the champion racing barge, the *Phoenician,* made no attempt to move.

As the *Northdown* and *Oceanic* went ranting out of the harbour, setting topsails at the pier-heads, we found that there was but a moderate sea outside. As the two vessels reached away towards Lowestoft I could see Eastland and his mate, who was a smart young fellow out of the local fishing smacks, working like demons to get the canvas on her. They got their boltsprit down before we did and drew ahead about a quarter of a mile. But once we had got our sails in proper trim we surged up on his weather quarter and it became plain that the *Northdown* was travelling the faster of the two. Moving through the swell like a thoroughbred she passed the iron-pot and went further and further ahead.

Five hours after leaving Yarmouth we were off Harwich with nearly fifty miles of the journey behind us; but the skies looked black and threatening. I hauled the *Northdown* close under the lee

Barge traffic on Long Reach at the turn of the 20th Century.
Note the 'stackie' laden with hay.

'Starvation roads' – barges waiting for orders in the hungry thirties.
The furled sails bespeak an optimism that times will not get
so lean that the vessels need be laid-up.

Cambria 'ramping' – deep laden, driving to weather with her rail awash.

The author at the helm of *Cambria* in snowy weather. From a barge-master's point of view, no weather was worse than a blizzard at sea.

Martinet, the last wooden 'boomie', at anchor.
Later vessels were rigged with sprits but no booms or gaffs.

Greenhithe, an 'iron pot', under full canvas.

Sara and *Veronica* racing. Besides these two exceptionally fast boats,
Everard owned a third – *Dreadnought*. London & Rochester's *Sirdar* was
the only other racing barge in the same league.

Attending to *Sara*'s headsails during a race.
The author is the second man from the left on the bowsprit.

of the land and was considering the pros and cons of being a bit more cautious than usual and of going into Harwich until the wind eased down. After all, we had accomplished the worst part of the passage and we could always get to London River from Harwich, even if we had to turn to windward the whole way.

While we were holding in towards the land Eastland saw his opportunity of making up lost ground and beating the *Northdown* to London. He was some miles astern but well in sight.

Cracking on every stitch she would bear, he kept her off outside the Cork in the best of the tide and cut across the Stone Banks into the Wallet. Heavy weather did not worry him as much as it did me because, being an iron pot, he did not have to think about the prospects of pumping.

We, in the meantime, were travelling slower than the *Oceanic,* being in the slack tide and also under the lee of the land. But when I saw her tearing across the Stone Banks I forgot all about my ideas of going into Harwich and cursed myself for not taking a chance and keeping offshore as Eastland had done.

With full mainsail we bore up for the Naze and bolted across the shallows at breakneck speed. We had wasted valuable time, but if we could get out into the strong flood tide again before the *Oceanic* got ahead of us we could still run away from her. We should never hear the last of it if the *Oceanic* beat the famous *Northdown.*

We came out into the Wallet about a couple of hundred yards ahead. Eastland was steering as straight as a die and I knew that he must be working hard at the wheel. You didn't need any jerseys on to keep you warm if you wanted to steer her on a good course in a strong wind.

Had the two barges been of equal speed Eastland would have beaten us, but the speed of the *Northdown* was too much for the *Oceanic.* We gradually drew ahead, the iron pot dropping further and further astern until, shortly after dark, we lost sight of his side-lights. By this time we were over the Spitway and splashing up-swin over the ebb. We brought up off the Ship and Lobster tavern at Gravesend at two o'clock in the morning, well satisfied with a sixteen-hours' passage from Yarmouth. Two hours later the *Oceanic* slid silently by on her way up to Grays, where she belonged.

Chapter Nine

THE YEARS SLIP BY very quickly in a sailing barge. Probably it is because the life is so full of interest, activity and variety. The humdrum existence of many landsmen, or even deep-sea steamboat men, seems dreadfully dull by comparison. With their regular hours, set habits and often uncongenial or monotonous employment, they cannot look back through the years and distinguish one day from another. The sailorman can remember (as long as his faculties allow) almost every day of his working life. For him the annual battle with the winter—the long, dark nights, the gales and fogs and cold—is followed by the welcome weather of springtime, coming like a sigh of relief to a hard-pressed traveller. The quiet, almost desolate, tidal creeks, with their rural surroundings and country pubs, contrast sharply with the openness of the North Sea or the blue-and-white beauty of the Channel coast, or the bustling industry of London River.

Time makes its impression on a sailorman only in a seasonal sense. There is no daily, clockwork routine to blind him to a full appreciation of his existence.

This hard and vigorous life has schooled a breed of men whose toughness, energy and resource is unequalled among the present seafaring population of the British coasts. If a man leaves the barges and takes up any other form of work one can pick him out in an instant. He retains that bull-like force and vigour, is not easily rattled and invariably shows a touch of a deep, dry humour which is typical of many a sailorman.

What happens to them? Some gravitate to the docks and wharves of the smaller ports and a skipper is reckoned fortunate indeed if his cargo has been stowed by ex-bargemen. He will get the maximum weight in his ship and have her in perfect trim without any trouble or worry. In fact he can safely go home for a couple of days until the loading is finished.

Here and there one finds ex-bargemen in jobs requiring quite a lot of organisation and planning, such as supervising the working of a company's craft, or who have become owners in a small way themselves. More often, as is natural, they are to be found as masters and mates of motor and steam vessels trading round the coast and across to the Continent. A man who can say 'I was in the barges' commands a certain amount of respect aboard any ship, though not, of course, from the fancy lads of the fashionable liners.

But whatever they become, bargemen can always be distinguished by their ways, their talk, their gait, and their physical strength. I feel quite proud to be able to say that I have known, as personal friends both ashore and afloat, some of the cream of coastal sailing masters; but never would I dare to pick out any one, or even a dozen, who could be said to be better than the others. Some are particularly proficient in one branch of barging and some in another. For it must be remembered that, while some bargemen never go further down London River than Southend, others can slash their way north to the Tyne or westward to the ports of Cornwall without so much as a glance at the chart.

That does not mean that the latter class are superior bargemen. They are, perhaps, better all-round seamen but river men could quite likely give them points on the finer arts of smooth water sailing and manoeuvring in close quarters.

Most bargemen, however, have been well schooled in tidal river work before they ever go coasting, and this knowledge serves them well even in places where they are comparative strangers.

If I were compelled to name a grand old man of sailing barges at the time this book is written I would, after no small amount of hesitation, confer such a title upon the present master of the *Geisha,* George Mead of Grays. Without saying that he is the best bargeman afloat (he would be the first to deny that), it is safe to say that no one knows more about coasting or river work, about the rigging and sailing of a spritsail barge, or about the tides and weather required to make a passage to any port on either side of the North Sea and Channel. And from what I know of bargemen not one of them would grudge him the crown. A man must have lived a pretty good life for his fellow beings to say that they have never heard a word spoken against him. That is what they say about George Mead.

He is over seventy now, and as I sat with him over a pint in the Bull at Ipswich he told me he had been barging ever since he was eleven years of age.

He is everyone's friend, and his weatherbeaten old face, surmounted by an old-fashioned moustache, has a smile and a laugh even in the times of greatest adversity. No sailorman, young or old, would be ashamed to ask advice of George Mead; and such advice would be given in so helpful and kindly a way that in the end the doubtful one would be convinced that there was nothing to doubt about. George would never set himself up as the great know-all, but had a way of convincing anyone in difficulty that he could come through by his own knowledge and enterprise and that anything George told him was superfluous and incidental.

His forecasting of wind and weather was so far beyond reproach that any thing contrary to his opinion from the Meteorological Office or the B.B.C. could safely be consigned to the cabin fire. I have known many a skipper trust his ship to George's judgement of to-morrow's weather.

George has seen good times and bad in spritty barges. He often talks of the hungry old days when he used to trade down-Channel, paid by the share. Freights were low, even for long passages, and many has been the time when potatoes have formed the main diet of the crew for the last part of the voyage. The crews did not always earn enough to buy a decent stock of food for the whole trip.

He can tell many a yarn of turning to windward up the Channel, homeward bound in an empty ship after an unprofitable voyage, with no money in his pocket and the grub locker almost bare. Every time the barge was put about and the foresail slogged across the fore horse the noise seemed to say 'Nothin' to come, nothin' to come, nothin' to come'.

George Mead worked his way up from boy to be master of the steel-built *Servic,* the finest class of coasting barge of her time, carrying two hundred and fifty tons to sea without being deeply laden. When I first knew him he had come out of the 'big 'uns' because of his advancing years and had charge of the 180-ton *Grecian,* which was blown to Holland and wrecked in the great November gale which we had survived in the *Northdown.* George and his mate were saved by the Aldeburgh lifeboat.

To compensate for the hardships of his early days at sea George could also recall the better days of ample work and reasonable freightage when a master who had his wits about him could earn enough to provide for his old age. He did well, too, in the first Great War, when cargoes of coal and coke were sailed across to France at fantastic rates of pay.

He is now content to sail the river and estuary in the little *Geisha,* trading between London, Ipswich and the Medway. As a fine character and a real gentleman I have never met the equal, ashore or afloat, of Skipper George Mead. May he have a fair wind and smooth passage for the rest of his days! He deserves it.

Chapter Ten

OUR LAST TRIP in the *Northdown* was from London to the Isle of Wight, carrying a mixed cargo of oil cake, bran and middlings up the Medina River to Newport.

We started in a southerly gale which kept us from going further than the Yantlet buoy in Sea Reach. A few days later we had to shelter from another bad spell in the East Swale River, not many miles further on. When we eventually ventured as far as the Downs the wind flew into the northwest with a vengeance and we had to ride out another 'spoon drifter' to our anchor off Deal.

The *Celtic*, a big two hundred and fifty tons iron pot, was in our company and bound to the same place. She took refuge in Dover harbour. But I was never a lover of Dover harbour on a down-Channel passage and preferred lying under the lee of the land in the Small Downs a little to the north of Deal pier. If the wind southered we could go back round the North Foreland and lie in Margate Roads. We had miles of grub and plenty of coal for the cabin fire. My belief at the time was that the wind would veer to the north.

After four days of rolling and pitching to forty-five fathoms of chain we hove up our anchor and wallowed away past Dover with a light breeze coming down from the North Foreland. Poor old Jimmy Burrell, skipper of the *Celtic*, being under the lee of the high cliffs in the harbour, did not have enough wind to get out. So we caused him to go in for a lot of bad language and arrived off Cowes a day ahead of him.

It was March, and Cowes was just beginning to stir from its winter slumbers. The yacht crews were assembling and the shapely hulls in the yards were being got ready for the delight of their owners. But there was a difference from other years when I have seen Cowes spring to life at the change of season with a veritable flurry of industry and enthusiasm.

There were not so many professionals in the town. The yards were not getting going as they generally did. Many of the bigger vessels were being left untouched. And from over the water, from the east side, came the noise of riveters and welders building long grey ships of war. It was this sound which overwhelmed the fitting-out atmosphere of the Cowes of old.

Old Toby, the huffler, came down the river to meet us off the Medina cement works and took the wheel as we boxed and twisted the barge round the little withies which marked the narrow, winding creek leading to the quay. There was a deal of pushing and shoving to do with setting booms and in the end we had to heave her up on to the mud berth by means of a wire run off to the shore and led round our windlass. There was not enough water to get right along-side and we had to lie some ten feet from our destination for three days until the tides were big enough to float the *Northdown* alongside.

• • • • •

It happened that about this time I had been receiving letters and telegrams from a firm of London shipowners asking me to take charge of a boom-rigged ketch barge named the *Martinet,* a fine old wooden vessel built at Rye in 1912, carrying 210 tons to her marks. She was a beautiful model with a clipper bow, shapely counter and heavy standing bowsprit. Many a time had she commanded my admiration, for not only was she a fine barge but also the nearest thing to the schooners I had sailed in years before.

She had two main vices as far as I knew then. She was equipped with a dangerous patent contraption for an anchor windlass—and she was reputed to be haunted.

This tale of being haunted was not to be laughed at, for it meant that many sailormen would not serve in her; and a fine ship with no crew is worse than no ship at all.

She lay off Greenhithe in London River without a crew while we were down at the Isle of Wight in the *Northdown.* One old sailor refused duty rather than sleep aboard her alone at night. He did so once and said he never would again.

According to his story 'old Carter', one of her previous skippers who had died aboard years before, got out of his bunk in the night, walked forward and gave her some more chain just as there was a strong wind getting up.

'I was lying on the locker,' the old timer said (it was more than he dare do to take off his clothes and sleep in one of the bunks) 'and kept quite still. I didn't know what old Carter would do if he found me there.'

Apparently Old Carter then came below again, satisfied that his anchor was holding all right, and nothing more happened. But the old sailor never set foot aboard the *Martinet* after dark again.

It was certainly a strange thing that death and misfortune had accompanied the *Martinet* all her life. In her early days she had shifted on the blocks and killed a shipwright; old Carter went to sleep in his bunk never to awaken; she had knocked out all her crew off the Whiting bank near Orfordness, in a heavy sea while they were getting the anchor up. On this last occasion the skipper, Billy Burrows, had his arm smashed so badly that eventually he died of it. Another skipper, after a long chapter of bad luck and accidents, went crazy and died a sudden death.

Yes, the devil was in her all right and she had an evil reputation. But she was lovely to look at. I liked her and I wanted her.

As events turned out the *Northdown* fell upon hard times. There was little or no work to be found for her unless I consented to descend to the ballast and rough stuff trades. And that, in a vessel like the *Northdown,* I would not do. I was discouraged at the thought that the owners were willing to have a beautiful barge like the *Northdown,* which should have been champion of all coasters, wracked and strained by loading wet mud from the dredger in Sea Reach and humiliated by carrying the stinking garbage of London to Sittingbourne.

On top of all that I fell ill on the way home from Newport and had to stay ashore for a couple of weeks. When I was well again, there still being no work worth doing for the *Northdown,* I succumbed to the wiles of the *Martinet.*

I remember well the day I stepped aboard her as she lay to the mooring buoy off Greenhithe. Harry came with me as mate and we found she had a cook still on the articles.

After a good look round her and an inspection of everything possible, including the condition of the sails (which were not too good), I stood on her deck and muttered to myself:

'Well, you're a fine ship but don't forget I'll kill you before you kill me. So you had better know who's going to be boss.'

No sooner had I spoken than to my amazement the ship answered me. Evidently she didn't like being talked to like that. At that very instant a flush of tide caught her head and she snapped her starboard mooring wire and lurched heavily against

a harmless little river barge tied up alongside, giving her a
vicious clout that brought her skipper and mate scurrying out on
deck to see what was the matter.

That was the *Martinet's* way of showing her temper. The
devil in her was very much alive.

Harry and I shackled the second anchor chain to the buoy in
place of the broken wire and sculled ashore to the White Hart,
considerably impressed by the behaviour of our new ship.

People in harbour pubs used to tell me: 'She'll have you, Bob,
if you stay in her. She'll do you in or maim you same as she done
to poor old Billy Burrows and all the rest of 'em.'

To which I could only reply, time and again, 'I'll kill her before
she kills me.'

Well, she did try to kill me. She tried to crush me against the
quay at Northam Bridge in Southampton; she tried to throw me
off the main gaff going round Orfordness; she bashed me in the
face with a windlass handle in Corton Roads; she had every man
jack of us laid out with some sort of fever at the height of a south-
west gale off the Gunfleet sands; she smashed three fingers of my
right hand, for which I suffer to this day. She tried to drown me on
a bitter winter's night—but in the end it was I who killed her. I
drowned her, just as she had done to others and tried to do to me.

I lived and sailed in that ship for two years but before I tell of
her final death struggle there are other things to be set down, for
great events happened while I was in the *Martinet.*

Our first cargo in her was from London to Poole, which was
homeward bound for me. Poole was the port I had first sailed out
of as a boy and the idea of going back there as master of the
Martinet filled me with no small amount of pride. Of course I had
forgotten that I had been away from there for many years and
when we arrived no one knew me from Adam.

We sailed up London River to Charlton for the first part of this
cargo. We were to take a hundred tons of rice meal out of a big
steamship lying there. I remember the remarks of the dockees as
we sheered alongside with our boom sails and arrogant bowsprit
making us look a real old timer among the modern ships and craft.

'Gawd blimey,' one of them said, 'look 'ere Bert. 'Ere's
Nelson's bleedin' ship.'

And Bert popped his head up out of the hatchway of a lighter
and said: 'Strewth! Who's goin' to stow 'er? Look at 'er little

hatches. She's all blinkin' deck.'

They did not like vessels with a lot of deck space and small hatches because it meant that the cargo had to be humped a long way into the wings. They liked large hatch-ways and very little deck space, like the big dumb lighters. It made work much easier for them. It did not matter to them that a ship at sea in bad weather is a great deal safer with the smallest possible hatchways.

'We don't want her here,' some of them called out. 'Take her away skipper. They want her up the Museum.'

I became used to all this banter and before we had been in the *Martinet* long Harry and I had all the answers ready. Harry, being a Cockney himself, had some particularly scathing replies which he used to rasp out with great effect on such occasions.

To the accompaniment of his cutting comments on dockers in general and the grumbling and swearing of the men, the bags of rice meal were pushed, shoved and lifted under our wings and midship decks. I had fifty tons stowed forward and fifty aft, leaving the middle bay of the main hold clear to take in eighty tons of cement from a wharf down in Long Reach.

We were finished before evening and, with a rude farewell from the dockers, we set our canvas to the westerly breeze and blew majestically away from this hubbub and rabble to berth alongside the cement jetty a few hours later. The night shift cement men loaded our eighty tons that night.

The next day was a Saturday and to our delight the wind shifted into the north. Away we reached down past Tilbury and Gravesend and through the Lower Hope into Sea Reach. By the time we arrived off Chapman Head the flood tide had begun to flow and we anchored on the edge of the sand shelf that silts out from the eastern end of Canvey Island.

High water was at ten o'clock that night; and a very black night it was. But a northerly wind is a blessing not to be missed by a sailorman bound down-Channel. So we had a cup of cocoa and Harry lit the side-lights. We could hardly see more than a few feet in front of us as we hove the anchor chain short and set the mainsail.

The cook wasn't very happy at the prospect of putting to sea on a pitch black night and I could soon tell that, although he was a willing worker, he was no great shakes as a seaman. It doesn't take long to find that out in a sailing ship, even in the dark. He had been in the *Martinet* three weeks before Harry and I joined her. He was a lanky individual who went by the name of Long Bert and had been a sailor on the English coast, an engineer in a deep-sea ship and a soldier in India. That is, if what he told us was true. I would not for one moment accuse him of being the world's greatest liar, but after a time we never believed anything he told us about his early life and adventures. He was about thirty years old, yet, when one day I reckoned up the years he was supposed to have spent at this, that and the other, I could not make him anything less than ninety-five!

But he was quite a good cook and kept the galley and living quarters clean, which is what a third hand is for in a sailing barge. In return for this I paid him thirty shillings a week, provided his food and occasionally lent a tolerant ear to his yarn spinning. He knew practically nothing about sailing and made not the slightest progress towards learning to steer, even with a fair wind on the quarter.

By the time the after canvas was set and the anchor aweigh our eyes were getting used to the blackness of the night. As she cast away on the port tack her lofty spars and white sails, against the glimmer of the stars, gave her a ghostly and romantic appearance.

For all her bad reputation the *Martinet* served us well on this, our first, voyage. The wind hung from the north so that we could stretch away down the estuary through the Princes Channel, steering from light to light and threshing along at a good pace. She had quite a turn of speed for her type, and later we found that she could outpace many spritsail barges on a broad reach. It was only when close-hauled that they beat her, for they sailed so much closer to the wind.

I stood at the wheel all night and at daybreak we were off the North Foreland. Harry gave me a spell while I had breakfast and a nap and the old ship, with booms squared off, hustled along inside the Goodwins, gybing over without any trouble at the South Foreland. Our luck was in. Before we were past the low sandy headland of Dungeness the wind shifted to a smart north-east breeze. With sheets slacked off and all sails drawing she sped down along the Channel coast like a seagull.

We periodically tried the pumps but she seemed to make only a little water; perhaps that was because I had taken care not to put a full cargo in her until I knew what she was like.

And when the warm sun came out (it was springtime) I felt that we had made a really splendid start in our new ship. It was a glorious passage—a fair wind all the way, fine weather; and the Channel coast looking its best in new April clothes. Times like these are consolation for the more grim and exacting aspects of a bargeman's life.

Of course there was work to do. Between times of steering, trimming sheets and cooking, we started getting some of the old paint off the bulwarks, renewing some of the ragged serving on the standing rigging, altering this and that and thinking out a few improvements in her running gear. But on such passages everything is a pleasure and there is no such thing as hard and monotonous work.

Darkness came over us off Beachy Head and a French fisherman from Caen chucked twenty fine scallops on our deck to show his gratitude for our giving him his course and distance from Rye Bay. They made a luxurious breakfast the next morning.

During the night Harry and I each slept three hours at a time. We always work these three-hour watches on the Channel runs, as three hours is reckoned quite a good 'night in' among sailing men. When I hear of steamship men being paid overtime if they do not get their full watch below I realise how out-of-date and old-fashioned my sea training has been. I do not blame them, but only reflect with wonderment how different things are nowadays.

All through the night we sailed pleasantly westwards, and in the morning haze we could see the cliffs of Ventnor on the Isle of Wight. As we passed quietly along by its southern shores the *Martinet,* her sails swaying easily against a background of blue and white sky, seemed to fit in with the beauty and peacefulness of the scene. The wind was still fair, the sun shone out again, the gulls swooped and swerved gracefully over and around us. There was only a gentle swell on the water and the sea looked very blue.

I thought of the poor shore folk catching trains to their factories and offices, herded into great cities and towns like so many ants, bustling, working and planning feverishly—and in the end most of them falling into the same old rut. I was fortunate indeed to be sitting on the quarter rail inbibing a mug of steaming tea, feeling the wind and sun on my face and limbs and with the tang of sea salt in my nostrils.

I was master of my own little world—and a very pleasant little world at that—doing a useful job of work for the community, earning a decent living, and using only the elements of nature to get me from one place to another.

Few men are content with the work they are compelled to do, but on that particular morning I was well content with mine. The mate, half leaning on the weather spokes of the wheel, was apparently meditating much on the same lines as myself.

'Barging would be a fine job if it wasn't for the owners,' he remarked with a sigh. 'They ought to let us take the cargo to anywhere we fancied.'

'Ah, but you've got to have owners to have barges,' I said, though inclined to sympathise with his point of view.

Harry was silent for a moment, gazed lazily aloft, sighed again, and concluded his reverie by saying:

'Well, it's a damn good job we're not trucked up with them out here, because I do enjoy a morning at sea like this.'

And with that profound observation he went below to a breakfast of porridge and bacon and eggs.

It was Monday, and on that afternoon we sighted Poole Bar buoy—hard to spy out from a distance as it is engulfed in the massiveness of Ballard Down.

In main sheet; down port lee-board; and we hauled the *Martinet* close to the wind to get through the narrow Swash Channel which leads round the shingle banks to the entrance of Poole Harbour.

It is a narrow entrance, between two sandy spits, but once inside there is to be seen (if you have time to take your attention for a moment from the business of entering) the loveliness of a great inland lake. In the centre there sits like a queen the beautiful island of Brownsea and on the mainland there are majestic pine trees, sand dunes, meadows and fascinating little creeks and beaches. But, of course, much of this natural beauty has been scarred by erections which serve as boarding houses, rich men's villas and small bungalows of the not-so-rich.

Hundreds of yachts, big and small, elegant and ugly, occupy the fairways and anchorages. Some of these are little more than week-end houseboats and voyage but a few meagre miles in sheltered water from one year's end to another.

Some of them, of course, are fine sailing vessels and with mixed crews of amateurs and professionals are handled with great skill and dexterity. In fact, a few of the amateurs (but only a few) are quite as good as the professionals, who have not had the practical schooling in seamanship which their forefathers had to go through.

Others just blunder about in a world of innocence and bliss, get in other people's way, and are a thundering nuisance to the likes of us.

We had to turn to windward in short tacks through the main channel which runs round the eastern edge of the harbour to the town quays. With yachts anchored and moored all over the place this was a task enough to give anyone a nervous breakdown. It meant that sometimes I had to judge our boards to a matter of a few feet and box the ship round sharply in time to draw clear of the next one.

The skill and judgement of the mate forward is a big factor on such occasions. If he lets go the bowline too soon the ship may gather way quickly and hit the next yacht, or if he lets it go too late she might pay off too far from the wind, lose way, and clout the craft you are going about to avoid. Likewise the handling of the jib sheets, which he has to do at the same time, can make a tremendous difference to the amount of way the ship retains and the consequent effect on the helm. All this he does by watching the swing of the stern, the speed of the ship as she comes up into the wind, the direction of the wind and any fluky puffs off high ground or waterside buildings, and the weight of the pull in the headsheets.

There is no time for orders from aft—the skipper is too busy judging his distance and attending to the wheel, main sheet, mizzen sheet and lee-boards. Each man is too busy to look at what the other is doing, but if both know their jobs and have confidence in each other all will go well—because nothing is attempted that the ship cannot do.

As our bowsprit swept over the deck of one yacht anchored in the narrowest part of the fairway, a smartly dressed woman in the cockpit casually remarked:

'Oh, look, George. Here's a big sailing ship going by.'

To which the worthy George replied enthusiastically:

'By Jove! She looks a fine sight. Good morning, skippah'.

This last he added with a cheery wave of his hand.

Harry was bursting to tell him what he thought of him lying in the fairway and so was I. If he hadn't had a woman with him he would have got a mouthful. It was a near shave and one more of my hairs went grey.

I always think that yachtsmen on the whole are a particularly jolly and sociable crowd. When I have dined and wined with them and sailed with them (as a sort of busman's holiday) I have often been set wondering if there is not some strange spirit which invades a man's being once he had tasted the joys of handling a sailing craft, however small she might be, for those whom I have met aboard their own boats and in their own clubhouses seem to be the most companionable and easy going of fellows, entirely devoid of pettiness or snobbery. They are interested in anything that sails and, apart from yachts, are keen to learn about the old sailing ships, schooners, fishing smacks and barges.

But alas, there are some among them who are blissfully

ignorant of the finer points of handling ships and boats, especially in a tideway or in strong winds. They have no real idea of the danger, damage and costly delay they can cause to vessels trading on their lawful occasions. It is a fact that the veriest ass can climb aboard a yacht and go careering about under the noses of ships, and possibly causing fatal collisions, without any law to prevent him.

I remember, many years ago, when I was mate with Eastland in the *Oceanic,* we were turning to windward up London River on the last hour of the flood tide, trying to save our high water into the Albert Dock. There was a cargo for us there out of a big ship which was short of overside craft and due to leave. We, on the other hand, had been idle for some time and were in need of work. So it was essential for us, the barge, the big ship and the stevedores that we dock on that high water.

A small one-man yacht was also beating up with us and continually crossed us on the starboard tack when the *Oceanic* was on the port tack. Although his yacht was not much bigger than our lifeboat he always stood on and forced us to give way. (It is laid-down by international law that a sailing vessel on the port tack must give way to a vessel on the starboard tack.) Several times this put us in awkward positions because the yachtsman, in sticking to his rights, did not appreciate that the *Oceanic,* by no means a handy vessel when empty, would not spin round like his little boat.

There was plenty of traffic going up and down and once, between two big steamships, we had to bear right away and gybe round; later, when he put us round again I had to drop the foresail down to prevent the barge going head first at a collier coming away from a wharf in Barking Reach. Much of that and we should never have saved either our tide into the dock or the resultant cargo. And the big ship would have been held up, too.

Probably the yachtsman did not mean to cause a lot of trouble and he had no doubt read in a book that while he was on the starboard tack he had right of way. But he did not take into consideration (through sheer ignorance) the amount of work and worry he caused the crew of a big, unhandy coasting barge; or that he was on pleasure bent and that we were after our bread and butter.

All the time Eastland's temper had been slowly coming to the boil. Once more he eased his helm down and gave way, but this time he shouted out to the yachtsman:

'If you do that again I'll bloody well run over you. I've got to be in the Albert this tide.'

Well, he did do it again; but Eastland held the *Oceanic* ramping full and let her go straight for the yacht. If we had hit her (and Eastland was a very determined man) both yacht and yachtsman would have been sent to the bottom. Perhaps Eastland would have shifted his helm and only struck her a glancing blow. I don't know. His patience was exhausted.

Anyway, the yacht hastily went about at the last minute and our mizzen boom scraped across his forestay as we went careering by. The yachtsman looked both alarmed and indignant.

Eastland leaned over the quarter rail, right over the other man's head, and said something to him which I cannot repeat here.

But I must get back to my story of the *Martinet*.

We reached Poole quay about seven in the evening, which concluded what might be termed a reasonably smart passage from London. A little crowd watched us moor up. Sails were given a harbour stow, hatches cleared, discharging gear rigged and off we went to the Poole Arms opposite. We felt that, apart from the passage, threading through all those gilded and expensive yachts without so much as giving one a playful bump was worth a pint—perhaps two.

Chapter Eleven

POOLE IS A HOMELY LITTLE PORT. In the evenings families stroll up and down the quay looking at the ships and out over their lovely harbour; coasters scuffle in and out with their coal, cement and oil; occasionally schooners and barges give the place an air of antiquity in keeping with the rambling old pubs and buildings facing the water. The ordinary folk there are very good-hearted when you get to know them and Poole has produced some of the toughest and roughest sea-dogs that have ever wetted their feet in salt water.

I have never met a sailor yet who did not like Poole. More than one from 'foreign' parts on the East Coast has settled down there in his declining years. The local fishermen and coasting sailormen lend a strong flavour of salt water about the talk in the local taverns.

The *Martinet* soon attracted the interest and attention of the waterside. As she was the last of the boomies, old fellows with red faces and bright blue eyes came along to have a yarn and remind themselves of the days when they sailed in similar craft. Youngsters stood about to stare at us as they might at some antique: and the older women-folk were vaguely reminded of 'the sort of thing grandfather went to sea in.'

While the cargo was being hove out the wind held in the north-east, but on the very last day of discharging it fell to a calm and then blew westerly. What unheard-of luck!

On the morning after we were finished we scrambled the sail on to her and dodged out through the gleaming brass knobs and white enamel of the yachts and squared off through the Looe gutway into Poole Bay, which is sometimes wrongly named as Bournemouth Bay. It was Poole Bay before there was ever such a place as Bournemouth.

It seemed that nothing could mar our good fortune. All the way up-Channel the wind remained westerly. When we reached the Downs it southered far enough for us to fetch up through the Gore and Four Fathom channels (in the southern part of the Thames estuary) on the port tack so that we anchored again off Greenhithe nine and a half days after we had left that part of the river for Poole.

There was no small degree of surprise in the White Hart Inn that we were back so soon. Some had looked upon the *Martinet* as about done for, what with her bad luck and accidents, and few expected to see her making fast passages again. Others said it was just a bit of luck (which was largely correct), but we soon proved that we could keep the *Martinet* up to a pretty good average.

We loaded for Poole again—the same sort of cargo—and went there and back in eleven days. But the *Martinet* didn't like being driven. She hadn't tried her devil tricks with us in earnest. In fact I was beginning to believe that the vile streak she was supposed to have was a lot of baloney.

It was on the way back from this second trip to Poole that she struck her first blow.

We were at anchor off Ramsgate, awaiting the tide to take us round the North Foreland. We had to muster at six o'clock in the morning because only the last hour or two of the ebb was required so that we picked up the first of the flood tide going up along the Kentish shore into London River.

Being a May morning, it was daylight at that time and, after a cup of tea, we set about heaving up our anchor. There was only a light, variable breeze off the land but a slight swell was coming down from the North Sea. It was this swell that nearly ended the varied career of Long Bert as he was heaving away on the starboard handle of the windlass.

As I have already said, the windlass was a dangerous patent affair without enough pawls or teeth to stop the handles flying back almost half a turn when the anchor chain snubbed taught as the ship's head rose to the swell.

Long Bert, being in a somewhat jubilant mood, was singing lustily as he hove when the *Martinet* reared her bow sharply on a bit of extra swell and the ship sat back sharply to her chain. The windlass took the weight and the handles slashed back viciously. Before we realised what had happened Harry was on his back across the fore hatches and Long Bert lay groaning on the deck with blood pouring from a gash in the side of his head.

The *Martinet* was going to teach us a lesson.

I was the fortunate one of the three, for the handle was wrenched from my hands and I was left on my feet and unscathed.

Harry, though bruised and shaken, was on his feet in a moment; but Long Bert did not move. For a moment I thought he was dead, so much blood was coming from his head, soaking his clothes and even running into the scuppers.

We lifted him on to the hatches and Harry dashed aft for a bowl of water and the medical box. Together we bathed the wound and bandaged it up according to the 'Ship Captain's Medical Guide' (a venerable publication that has saved many a man's life at sea when he has had to depend on rough and unskilled attention).

For twenty minutes Long Bert lay inert before us. For twenty minutes I did not know whether he was going to live or die there on the hatches. There was nothing more we could do except keep him warm. No ships were near to signal for assistance. We were too far off from Ramsgate to get help from there.

While I was wracking my brain for the best thing to do a smart breeze came puffing from the east-south-east. The main canvas had been set before the accident occurred and when this breeze came I think it was the shaking of the sails that brought Long Bert back into the same world as us.

He lifted his head an inch of two, swore terribly at the windlass, and then fell back unconscious again. I felt thankful for even this brief return to life because I knew he wouldn't die if he could swear like that.

Soon he came round again and we were able to carry him aft and down into the cabin, explaining to him as briefly as possible what had happened. He seemed to want to know. Harry made him comfortable and plied him with warm tea.

I went on deck, struggled with the anchor and got the ship under way. I had intended to sail into Ramsgate Harbour and put our casualty ashore. But as we closed the land he improved rapidly, so that I squared away round the Foreland and up through the Gore. With a spring flood under us and an easterly wind we were soon at Greenhithe and Long Bert was packed off to hospital. That was the last we ever saw of him. I do not think he went to sea again.

When the population of the waterfront saw the bandaged man being helped ashore from the *Martinet* there was much muttering and shaking of heads in the local taverns. The *Martinet* was up to her old dirty tricks. She had got one of her new crew already.

'Poor chap,' they said, 'I suppose he didn't know what she was like.'

And it did seem (though I claim to be able to laugh at superstition) that there was some sort of evil spirit in her. She was strong and beautiful, but that wicked streak in her would keep coming out.

There was no cause to doubt it on the next voyage, which was to the little-known port of Wells in Norfolk. We went there with a cargo of oil-cake and this time the *Martinet* turned on me.

Sailing down by Hollesley Bay, between the Whiting Bank and the Suffolk shore, the wind veered to the northwest, which meant that we had to haul in our sheets as we passed the Ness.

The mate and the new cook, a strong young lad from another barge, were rounding in the mainsheet when I noticed that part of the lacing on the main gaff aloft was chafed through. Probably it had been rubbing on the back-stays when we had the wind aft.

There being one or two other items I wished to inspect aloft I thought I would go up and see to it all and repair the lacing at the same time.

Harry took the wheel while I clambered up the rigging and out on to the gently swinging gaff It was fine weather and it was an easy job for one brought up to such monkey-like activities. While I was knotting back the frayed ends of the lacing (which holds the sail to the spar) I sat on the gaff with one arm round the peak halliards (which hold the gaff aloft) so that I could work with two hands free. Being thus peacefully engaged, occasionally looking about me to enjoy the panorama of coastline and sunlit sea, my body was suddenly precipitated downwards with a violent jerk. I was saved from a headlong descent to the deck, some eighty feet below, by my hand becoming entangled in the lacing I had just repaired.

It was only small cordage but it held my weight while I reached up frantically with the other hand and grabbed the gaff span, a wire strop to which the peak halliards are shackled. I knew instantly that the peak halliard had slipped on the barrel of its winch on deck and thought that perhaps the new cook was meddling with it while I was up on the gaff.

Bursting to vituperate blindly and viciously at whoever it was, I edged my way back to the safety of the mainmast and came down on to the deck. When I looked round for the culprit there was none to be seen. Harry was standing serenely at the wheel and Joe was screwing himself up in the galley in an effort to clean out the cooking range. Neither of them had been near the winch.

My anger having been exploded into thin air, I went to the halliard winch and found that the pawl had broken off. The topsail sheet was holding the gaff up. If the topsail had not been set I should, almost certainly, have been killed.

I effected a temporary repair of the winch gear and dismissed the matter from my mind. It does not do to reflect too long on such incidents. But there did cross my mind the memory that in this very spot, Hollesley Bay, Billy Burrows had lost his right arm when he was skipper of the *Martinet.* And poor Billy had died. I, who had laughed at and doubted many of the old tales about the *Martinet,* was slightly shaken. I will confess to that much. After all, that sail had been set for over twelve hours and not until I went up on the gaff in Hollesley Bay did the pawl give way. My own bodily weight could not possibly have caused it to break. Normally it would stand the weight of a couple of dozen men at least.

Who dares to jeer at old seamen's tales when things like this happen at sea? But I soon forgot about it; what with having my hands full at sea and my tankard full when we got ashore at Wells. And it is a simple enough business to find one's tankard always full in that place, for rarely have I found such hospitable folk. I was a stranger there on the first day; knew half the town on the second; and on the third was carried off like an old friend on the annual outing of the Ship Tavern.

Three weeks we lay alongside the old quay, waiting for a change of wind to get to sea. For Wells is a queer sort of port. There are miles of sand between the harbour and the sea with only a narrow gutway, deep enough for a coaster to navigate when the tide is full, connecting the two.

At last we got the *Martinet* out of this rat-trap of a port with the aid of a local motor boat which was not powerful enough to tow us, but which helped to pull the barge's head round the sharp bends of the creek and get her about when she had not room to make a proper tack. I was glad to be done with all this when we finally cleared the little bar buoy and away we went on a long beat to windward in an empty ship.

There was no good fortune to be had that trip. We met a southerly gale in Yarmouth Roads and were days and days making thirty or forty miles. The *Martinet* was a poor thing when going to windward without any cargo in her. Her leeboards were not heavy enough, her sails too old and baggy and, being high-sided, she blew to leeward 'like a bladder of lard' as the Essexmen say.

We were off Southwold when the devil in her had another go at me.

We had made a long tack offshore and as we came about I picked up the pawl of the leeboard winch on the starboard side to let the board run down in the usual manner. It ran down all right but while it was doing so I slipped on the deck and two fingers of my right hand went between the spinning cog wheels of the winch. The top of one finger came off and the other was crushed into a sticky mess.

I quickly picked up the top off the deck and stuck it on again, holding it there until Harry had hove the vessel to and bandaged me up. It grew on and is there to this day, a numbed and frostbitten souvenir of the wicked old *Martinet*. The other finger also became stiff and subject to frostbite in succeeding winters.

Had the headwinds persisted I would have put into Harwich the next day and had the damage attended to by a doctor; but a spanking breeze came out of the north-east and it was too good to miss. We were fed up with headwinds and, since I was able to steer with one hand and an elbow while Harry and Joe did all the hard work, the smashed fingers had to wait until I got ashore at Greenhithe two days afterwards.

It had been an unlucky trip all round, for the freightage was very low and, having taken six weeks over the job, I had practically nothing to come. After paying the crew, buying stores, and losing the use of two fingers, I had exactly four shillings left for myself at the end of the voyage.

I was then placed on the sick list for a month at thirty bob a week and didn't feel very pleased about it. But it took that time for my injury to mend.

Meanwhile, Phil Finch, skipper of the racing barge *Sara* (which was under repair) took charge of the *Martinet* and loaded her with a cargo of middlings for Poole. She was towed down-Channel by one of the company's small steam-vessels. Phil Finch was a typical Essex bargeman—oldfashioned, jovial and partial to a pint. A merry old soul if ever there was one, and an excellent shipmate.

He was still on board the *Martinet* when I rejoined her at Poole, and remained with us until we had loaded a cargo of cement at Medina in the Isle of Wight and delivered it to the depot in Southampton.

Phil's main interest in life was barges, especially racing barges. He was one of a famous barge-racing family from the little village of Mistley, near Harwich. Oftimes he had raced in the *Sara* and many were the tales he had to tell of the schemes and dodges they used to get up to in trying to outwit their rivals in the annual matches.

There was a lot of yacht racing going on off Cowes while we were there, and Phil would have loved dearly to have set foot aboard one of those trim six-metres and tried out some of his old tricks against the amateur gentlemen.

Of all Phil's cheery tales of London River and his native Essex creeks there is one which I shall always remember.

He had a mate in the *Sara* by the name of Patsy—a good mate but very deaf. One day, when turning to windward up Long Reach, the barge was hit by a thunder-squall which was accompanied by torrential rain. Patsy, who was forward, took what shelter he could find under the lee of the mainmast, leaning back on the mainsail in an effort to keep dry.

The squall became worse than Phil expected and he yelled to Patsy to drop the head of the topsail down. The barge was beginning to stagger under the weight of the wind. But what with the noise of the wind and the rain and the peals of thunder, and Patsy being so deaf, he did not hear the shouts of his skipper.

Exasperated, Phil hastily locked the wheel, picked up a broom handle off the hatches, and ran forward to where the tempting profile of Patsy's backside could be seen pressing against the mainsail from the other side. The master of the *Sara* gave it a resounding thwack and in a trice was back at the wheel again.

Just at that moment there was a brilliant flash of lightning. Patsy came flying aft to where Phil stood steering as though nothing had happened. The mate was well and truly alarmed.

'Skipper, I've been struck. I've been struck by lightning.'

Phil rounded on him unsympathetically.

'Well, I've told you before not to stand by the mast in a thunderstorm. I've been yelling my guts out to tell you to shift. Now go and drop the head o' that topsail down before anything else happens to you.'

And to this day Patsy still believes that he was once struck by lightning in Long Reach.

We were sorry to lose old Phil's company, but my injuries had healed and he had orders to go back to his own ship. Before he left he wrote a letter to his wife which the mate inadvertently posted in the vicinity of Parkhurst Prison. The postmark caused much misgiving in his native village until he could get home and explained that he had been down-Channel in the *Martinet*.

Chapter Twelve

THIS WAS NOT intended to be a tale of war, but a description, clumsy though it may seem, of life in a sailing vessel trading on the English coast.

War came, the second world war of my lifetime, and it must needs butt into the story just as it butted in and upset so many millions of people's lives.

Being somewhat detached from the general mass of humanity in the thickly populated areas on shore, the effect of the declaration of war on sailormen was rather different, less profound and less awesome than on some people. We were used to a life of hazards and danger. This new war, whatever it might bring, was but an increase in the hazards and a decline in the safety factor of our occupation. Few of us but knew what it was to be short of food, to be ill-clad and even penniless at times, and yet still carry on with a job which was not to the fancy of such as might be fond of his comforts, or even of his skin.

I, like others, had in hard times appeased my famished body on a diet of potatoes and bread; shivered at night on the bare boards of a bunk for want of bedding; faced a North Sea blizzard with an empty stomach and clothes only fit for warm, sunny weather. And that part of my tale which has already been told will show that a sailorman is of a different metal, a different make up, has a different background and a different outlook from your ordinary citizen.

So the war did not come as a very great shock. Most of the skippers and mates of my acquaintance accepted the news rather stoically, content to carry on with their jobs and see how things turned out. In fact they were, without actually realising it, relying on their well-tried resourcefulness and adaptability to meet whatever circumstances the war might place them in.

Just before the German army (the very existence of which seemed to have been the cause of all modern wars) stamped into Poland, the good ship *Martinet* had just done a rapid series of voyages between Poole, Medina, Southampton, London and Yarmouth.

We left Poole light for Medina River and did the cargo of

cement, which Phil Finch helped us with, to Southampton. After Phil had gone home we bowled up-Channel with a bonny breeze on the quarter to Tilbury, to load there the day after arrival with a hundred and seventy-five tons of rice for Yarmouth.

We sailed on the evening of the day we loaded and towed into Yarmouth in time to have our dinner alongside the quay next day in company with the *Martha, Ethel Everard* and *Lady Maud*— exactly nine days from the time we had left Poole, including the days taken in loading and discharging. Even old Frank Day of the *Martha,* who was the perfect antidote to any form of flattery, admitted that we hadn't done too badly, although he supposed that we must have been very lucky with the tides and weather.

Back we went to London and loaded for Poole again, this time our customary cargo of rice meal and cement. While the fine summer weather lasted I was anxious to get down-Channel again and, as soon as the hatches were on, we got the canvas on her and tacked away down river against a light easterly breeze. I was hoping that it would freshen and blow us down to Poole once we had griped to windward round the North Foreland. But that was not to be.

Fog came in the morning, thick and sudden, descending like a mask over the estuary of the Thames. We were then edging down Sea Reach, working to windward along by the Yantlet sands, and the complete cessation of all visibility compelled me to try and get into the usual anchorage off Yantlet Creek, near which we were.

The fog was so dense that I could not even see the topsail; and the mate on the foredeck moved about like a ghostly wraith.

I sounded into *five* fathoms and gave the order to let go the anchor. As the chain rattled out through the hawse pipe the bow of a ship appeared in the rigging and struck us a shuddering blow by the main chain plates. Her sharp stem bit into our outer wale and, we being loaded almost to our marks, I feared that the *Martinet* might sink in a matter of a few minutes.

I thought at first that we had been hit by a ship coming up river, but it turned out that the other vessel had just let go her anchor and that the ebb tide had carried the *Martinet* on top of her just as we were bringing up ourselves.

There was a grim humour in the situation, for I looked up and saw the name *Prowess* on the bow of the other ship. She was one

of our own company's motor tankers and commanded by Barney
Seaman, who had served for years in the *Martinet* as well as
several of our other sailing barges. The *Martinet* had been his
first ship as a boy and he had walked her decks as cook, A.B.,
mate and master.

Barney looked over the bow to see what had happened.

'Well, I'll go to hell,' he cried, 'if it isn't the old *Martinet*. For
ten years I tried to run away from her and now she comes after
me in a fog.'

The hole in our side, though dangerous if there had been any
swell, was just above water. For a moment the *Martinet* was held
athwart the *Prowess* by the tide and then swung clear.

Harry and the cook picked our anchor up clear of the ground
while I hastily stuffed a sack in the hole and tried the pumps. I
was thankful to find that there was not any water in the bilges.

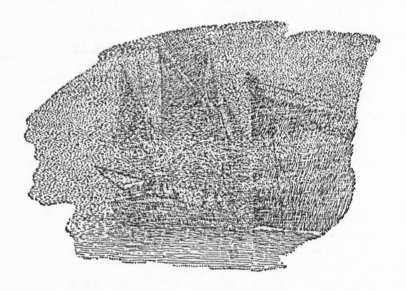

We anchored astern of Barney's ship, he shouting out to us
through the fog to know if we were all right; for as soon as the
vessels were a few yards apart each vanished from sight of the
other in the impenetrable blanket of white.

Fortunately our damage was not so serious as it might have
been had the hole been a few inches lower. We stuffed sacks and

canvas in it and nailed a deal board over the lot.

The outcome of all this trouble was that when the fog cleared some hours later Barney towed us back to the Greenhithe yard for repairs. It was while we were there that we heard the fatal news of war.

I was in the White Hart at the time, having a pint with old Phil Finch. Having listened patiently to the various ponderous announcements on the wireless we wondered how this new conflict would affect the sailing barges: for, like most people at that critical time, we thought first of our own personal affairs.

The great uncertainty was as to what the air raids would be like and whether the Germans would use gas bombs. The Germans had held their air weapon like a mailed fist in their dealings with all the countries in Europe. 'Give us what we want or we'll bomb you to bits' was the obvious and simple basis of German diplomacy. In fact that is the gist of what the German leaders told the British Prime Minister, Neville Chamberlain, during the latter's painstaking efforts to stave off and avoid a terrible war which inevitably brought hatred and suffering in its wake.

Yet this German way of dealing, though it may have struck fear into some, roused a stubborn defiance in the hearts of sturdier folk. For in all my travels, which in younger days took me by ship and sail to many far-off lands, I have never known a race or type so obstinate or stubborn as a thoroughbred Englishman, however poor his standing, in the face of a bully. And I say this with all due respect to the well-proved courage and gallantry of other British and Continental races of people. But mine is a humble opinion and formed largely from the qualities I have observed in tavern brawls, waterside feuds and such turmoils and violence as are often perpetrated in the low dives of seafaring towns abroad.

So it proved in the terrible trials to come that this English stubbornness came well to the fore when the common people stood their ground in the face of a cruel bombardment from the German airmen. How these Germans, for all their medieval barbarism, came upon a stumbling block of bitter endurance and defiance it is not my business to tell. But all the world knows how the brutal instigators of modern aerial bombardment of civilians were eventually repaid in their own kind.

When the *Martinet* had been repaired and we were once more ready for sea the owners thought it advisable that we should be

towed down to Poole by one of their steamers, the *Glen Mary,*
which was bound that way.

It was just as well, for we were short-handed. I had sacked the
cook because, apart from being lazy, he had such filthy habits as
were not conducive to a decent preparation of meals. No other
third hand being available, Harry and I were on our own.

We gave the *Glen Mary* our towing wire, which was shackled
to a ten-inch manilla hawser, which in turn was shackled on to
the first three fathoms of our second anchor chain.

Before sailing the master of the *Glen Mary* had to obtain
routeing instructions from the Admiralty, all shipping being now
under Naval control. I was provided with a copy also in case we
should break adrift, or get into trouble with the enemy, and have
to proceed under our own sail.

This Naval Control Service, though its personnel had every
good intention, eventually became the bane of my existence (and
that of all other sailing bargemen as well). Had the sailing
bargemen always obeyed their instructions their vessels would
have been of little or no use to the Ministry of War Transport.
Depending as they did on winds and tides, a point which the
Navy people could never seem fully to appreciate, the barges
could not have made regular passages and carried such important
cargoes as they did if the skippers had taken these Naval
instructions seriously.

We learned to obey them when it was easy to do so and when
they did not entail long detours, rank bad seamanship and costly
delays. But after the first few weeks of war we all came to look
upon these sheets and sheets of typewritten manuscript as so
much toilet paper.

The *Glen Mary* lugged us down to Poole bar buoy in almost
exactly twenty-four hours. There she let go our towing gear,
being bound further westward, and we came to anchor to await
the flood tide into the Haven entrance. By the time we had got all
the wire and rope aboard and stowed away, which was no easy
job for two hands, the ebb was done and we set the sails. It was a
long beat up to the quay but, thank Heaven, nearly all the yachts
had been taken out of the way and laid up for the duration of the
war.

As we were mooring up to the quay an old fisherman friend

told us that the Russian Army had marched into Poland. The war was getting a move on. We thought at the time that Russia, as well as Germany, was going to fight against us. Poland, our ally, was already on her knees.

The news was discussed in the pub that evening with considerable foreboding, for the Polish Army was being cut to pieces. The French had made a sort of reconnaissance expedition beyond their Maginot Line into the Warndt Forest, but had not attempted anything in the nature of an offensive which might counterbalance the success of the German Army in the east. France and Britain had not the numbers to withstand Germany and Russia too. Things looked black indeed.

While our cargo was being discharged I made a few enquiries to try and find a crew. My old friend Colombos, the Poole ship-chandler, said he might be able to send a man along, and our broker was also asked to get on the scent of any poor fool who wanted to go to sea in a sailing vessel.

One evening a nondescript individual came to the quay-side and gave us to understand that he wished to go to sea. He had never been on the water, never set foot on board a ship, had no idea what the life was like and knew nothing at all about seamanship. He had spent most of his time being employed in an amusement fair—taking money on roundabouts and the like.

This did not worry me a lot at the time. I was capable of being very hard-hearted at times. Here was a human being, apparently sound in wind and limb, who wanted to go to sea. We were short-handed. Once aboard he would have to work whether he liked it or not. He was big enough to pull on a rope, turn a windlass handle, scrub decks, wash dishes, peel potatoes, polish brass, use a paint brush, chop firewood, lift hatches, and generally make himself useful. If he didn't get on with it or proved a shirker I could kick him out when he got to London. So I signed him on. He came to be known as Freddie and had had a most varied career. He could operate a steam roller, drive a horse, work the 'dodgems' at the fair, swindle people out of their change (he demonstrated to me how this was done), cheat at cards, and often described the advantages and disadvantages of life in Wormwood Scrubs, Portland prison and various other places of detention.

He could scarcely read (apart from having a weird squint and very bad eyesight) but his one great boast was that he had once been co-librarian with a lord in prison. Freddie had a small, bullet head, narrow slit eyes and the general appearance of a typical convict. But I did not inquire too closely into his past. We were short-handed.

No sooner had I secured the services of this estimable person than along came old Colombos with a tall, good-looking fellow whom he introduced as George Vlasto. He was fortyish, cultured and friendly. He wanted to put in a few months at sea to qualify for a position in the Navy. They would not have him unless he had had some genuine sea-experience.

So Colombos had brought him to me with the confidential information that he was a nice chap, a real gentleman, but a good mixer and willing to rough it. All of which later proved to be true. In the end I signed him on, making the *Martinet* four-handed. Thus she came down-Channel with only two and was going back with four.

George had been a cavalry officer in India and I wondered how his virtue of being a good mixer was going to stand the strain of association in close quarters with such as the worthy Freddie.

I had a good chance to break in my new crew as we were fixed to load, for Queenborough, a cargo of china-clay, which needed a great deal of trimming. This clay was brought down in lighters from Wareham and some old chaps hoisted it aboard in skips (like big baskets). The crew had to trim the big slimy lumps under the decks and cupboards, and it was a job which either broke your back or broke your heart. So I set them at it, driven at a pace which the mate thought fit.

There were occasional sorties across the road to the Poole Arms but the work went on for ten hours a day.

By the end of the first day you could not tell the cavalry officer from the roundabout man as the pair of them dragged their aching bodies out of the hold, plastered from head to foot with a white slime. Their clothes, faces, and even their hair were white. Freddie stood up to the work the better of the two, for he was no stranger to a pick and shovel. But George was a sticker and not to be beaten and he got the knack of hard labour as time went on. So in the end we got the ship into excellent trim with one hundred and ninety tons loaded by hand in four days.

We were to be seen a good deal in the Poole Arms in the

evening. Whether this was due to trimming china-clay, the excellence of the beer, the friendly hospitality of the landlord and his wife, or to the blandishments of Lilian the barmaid I am not prepared to judge. But the fact remains that we all became very well known there and the landlady and several of her customers, and Lilian of course, volunteered to come and see us off at six o'clock in the morning, when we intended to put to sea.

The landlady made a special brawn for us which she said she would bring aboard at the aforesaid early hour, and one old fellow even asked the local lodging-house keeper to call him at five-thirty so that he could come and let go our ropes off the quay for us.

On the appointed morning, the vessel being loaded and battened down, our pub friends faithfully appeared on the quay as promised. The brawn was put aboard and the sleepy-eyed well-wishers felt that they had lived up to their promises.

But alas! The wind had flown into the east and we could not sail. So that night we all appeared in the pub again, saying that we expected to sail the next morning. The little concourse again mustered to see us off. Again the wind came easterly and we did not start.

This went on for four days until our friends got fed up with the idea. The brawn was eaten before we ever left the quay, and when we eventually got under way there was not a soul about to let go our ropes for us as we sheered away.

The *Glen Mary* had, during all this time, been down to the westward and come back to Poole. She was bound to London and had orders to tow us. I did not like the prospect of this, having now got a full crew, but such were the orders from the owners.

On the morning we left Poole the wind had shifted to the south-south-west and was blowing hard. The *Glen Mary,* being empty, blew about like a football and in attempting to tow us clear of the quay nearly went ashore on the mud at the edge of the Little Channel. In getting back into deeper water she dragged us round in a wide circle so that we narrowly missed wiping a group of small fishing boats off the face of the earth.

Eventually our tow rope got foul of our main anchor (owing to the inexperience of the crew) and all the *Glen Mary* could do, and that with difficulty, was to pull us out of the harbour into the open bay. Being then foot-loose and having a fair wind I implored

her skipper to let us go. Although he did not like leaving us, in
view of the owners' orders, we finally got rid of him, set the
canvas, and jogged along our own sweet way.

We were not long crossing Poole Bay and hauling to windward
of the Isle of Wight, for it was blowing a full gale. A heavy sea
was rolling up the Channel, slopping over our weather quarter
and burying the lee decks.

We soon missed our new crew and Harry found them leaning
over the stern behind the wheel-house, looking much worse than
when they were trimming clay, and practically incapable of any
form of word or movement. Although one was a cavalry officer
and one a roundabout man, it was obvious that sea-sickness was
a great social leveller. They occasionally sympathised with each
other and commented on what they had brought up.

'There goes the brawn,' George would mutter faintly.

'That's my last pint,' Freddie would rejoin sadly.

For purposes of working the ship Harry and I were two-
handed again. Our principal concern was to get a good offing, as
the wind was well on the land and too far southerly to give us a
comfortable run. All four lowers were kept on her to help hustle
her out to windward and when we were far enough offshore to
feel that we had 'a bit in hand' we snugged her down to mainsail
and jib. Away she ranted to the eastward, lurching like a
drunkard and steering like a haycart.

Harry joined me at the wheel as lee helmsman after the sail
shifting was done, for it was sometimes more than I could do to
keep her from yawing to windward and taking the seas broadside
over her weather rail. Off Worthing a wicked old fellow broke
over our quarter and smashed the boat in the davits. The next sea
washed away the broken parts and left us with the stem and stern
post still dangling in the tackles with no boat between.

The ship was careering along at about eight and a half knots
and I knew that Harry and I were in for a nice night. What had
happened to the other two and where they were was more than
we had time to worry about. We felt that they were sure to be
clinging to some part of the ship. Self-preservation is very strong,
even in brand-new mariners.

Before darkness came down Harry struggled with the wheel
alone while I went round the deck on reconnaisance. I wanted to

make sure that all the gear was sound, nothing chafing through or liable to break, to see that the canvas was standing the strain and the hatch wedges secure.

I came across Freddie, wet through and half dead with sickness, lying half in and half out of the lavatory aft, his trousers down round his boots and his chest sticky with vomit. George had had the presence of mind to provide himself with a bucket and crawl below.

Next Harry had a look round to make doubly sure that everything was all right before nightfall and he managed to bundle Freddie's inert body down the forecastle scuttle and pull the hatch over.

We did see George for a few minutes. Bravely he struggled up the companion ladder and said in a hollow voice, like one from another world:

'Do you require your able-bodied seaman, skipper?'

I said 'No' and he nodded thankfully and disappeared below again. It was good of him to offer!

All that night Harry and I steered the *Martinet* up-Channel. She tore along like a train. I remember him saying:

'If a German submarine wants to stop us now he'd better call again some other time.'

And that was all we thought of the war that night.

Wet through and tired, we prayed for the wind to wester. But the best it would do for us was to veer a couple of points to south-west. This made steering a little easier, and as dawn broke Harry went below for an hour's nap. Later he emerged with a steaming cup of tea, for which I blessed his heart as tenderly as any mother.

Thus invigorated, we faced the coming day in better heart. Harry roused our prostrate crew in his best bucko style. With many threats and oaths he propped the new cook up in the galley and told him that if he did not get on with cooking breakfast he'd knock his bullet head off. Vlasto, feeling better, turned out willingly enough and helped Harry to steer while I lay down for half an hour on the locker in the cabin.

Freddie produced the breakfast, which Harry and I promptly wolfed. The others could not bear the sight of it. By dinner-time the wind had eased considerably and the seas had lost their white crests. The worst was over and the weather started the fine-up.

In the afternoon we were toddling gently round the South

Foreland with the balloon foresail set, flying jib topsail and mizzen staysail. The mate and I took turns to indulge in a luxurious afternoon nap. George and Freddie came to life and gradually set about the resuscitation of their wasted bodies.

There were a lot of big steamers anchored in the Downs and a Naval Control Service tug hailed us and wanted to know all the details of our voyage. The officer in charge then ordered us to anchor in the Small Downs and warned us not to proceed round the North Foreland until we had been given permission.

How I swore! The wind was then south-east—a fair wind right round the Longnose and up the Estuary to Queenborough. It is not often a sailing vessel from the Channel gets a lucky slant like that. And now we had to bring up. The Navy ruled over all, fair winds or foul, and with bitter regret we had to let go our anchor, being thus denied at the last the fruits of our endeavours and hardships of the last twenty-four hours.

The wind freshened that night from the east-south-east and we had to pay out a good deal of chain as a steady swell was coming over the Goodwin Sands. Normally it is reckoned very bad seamanship for a sailing vessel to lie in the Downs with the wind in this direction, but the Navy people did not allow for that and we started to roll and pitch as darkness fell.

I lay in my bunk and thought how we might have been round the corner and up at Queenborough instead of facing the prospect of an anxious night wallowing about in this so-called anchorage. The *Martinet* might have been safely moored up to the buoy in Queenborough creek and the crew perhaps sitting comfortably alongside their pints in that friendly old pub at the top of the causeway called the Old House at Home.

Before morning I was awakened by a more violent motion of the vessel and went on deck to find a strong wind blowing straight on to the land. I called Harry and he mustered the hands to help get the second anchor ready. As the tide made to the southward I gave her a hard sheer to starboard, paying out sixty fathoms on the main anchor and then letting go the second. We hove back fifteen fathoms on the main and then paid out thirty on the second.

Thus we lay all that night and all next day, wondering when the Naval tug would come and tell us we could go. No one came near us though there were a number of Control tugs steaming about the anchorage.

The next night we had to give her more chain as the swell was getting bad. I did not like the look of things at all. And I could hardly speak a civil word to anyone when I thought that we might have been safe in our port of destination.

We had another rotten night and a deal of pumping to do. The snubbing and wallowing, with a lot of water coming over the decks, made the old *Martinet* strain and creak. We kept anchor and pump watches and the comments on the Naval Control Service would not bear repetition.

By morning I had reached the end of my tether and was in the right mood to talk to anyone, from the Admiral of the Fleet down, about making a sailing vessel lie in the Downs with an easterly wind for the sake of a lot of footling regulations dished out as though they were valuable by a bunch of ex-clerks in brass buttons.

I had all hands to the windlass to get the anchors and it was a long, hard job. By the time the second anchor was aboard and stowed and the main hove short we had done four hours heaving and sweating. We broke out, set all plain sail, and stood offshore.

There were then a number of Naval Control vessels cruising between the big steamers and I expected trouble right away for getting under way without permission. But not one of them came near us. So up went the topsail and we bore away for the North Foreland. They could go to hell with their orders for all I cared. I had learned my lesson. This book could be filled with the cunning evasion and trickery I eventually practised throughout the war to avoid all such red tape.

I could not help remembering what the old skippers at Ipswich had told me about their experiences in the last war with the Naval Control. I had thought they were exaggerating at the time, but I didn't after those forty-eight hours in the Downs!

We picked our way through the dimly-lighted Edinburgh Channel that night and ran up to the Nore, anchoring off the entrance to the Medway. In the morning we were plagued by a Naval Control vessel and told we must not enter the port until we had received instructions. We rolled about there all day waiting for instructions that never came. We had another uncomfortable night, the breeze having freshened from the east, sending a short steep sea up the Estuary, especially on the ebb tide.

Patience having given out again, I had the anchor hove up
next morning and sailed the barge into the river past Sheerness,
intending to get to Queenborough at all costs in spite of the
Naval Control Service, which seemed designed to prevent us
from getting anywhere. What was more serious was that we were
beginning to leak pretty badly with all this unnecessary buffeting,
and the crew were getting a bit weary of the pumps.

Although I had traded for some years up the Medway and its
creeks I was compelled by war regulations to engage a pilot to
take us in. He came aboard as we reached into the river and
insisted on taking the wheel. He was only a young chap and I
could see in a moment that he didn't know much about sailing a
barge. He nearly put us ashore in coming about off the entrance
to Queenborough creek, the wind having southered and drawn
down the river. So after a few diplomatic suggestions we let go
our anchor, put him ashore, and did the awkward bit without his
assistance.

Chapter Thirteen

OUR CARGO OF CLAY having been discharged and Queen-borough's special breed of rats chased off the ship, we sailed up to London and were soon fixed to load wheat for Norwich. Little did the merchants who bought the wheat suspect what a rough passage it was going to have. Neither did we.

All went well as we sailed gracefully and peacefully down Sea Reach and the West Swin in gloriously warm and sunny weather. It was a most encouraging start to a passage. The wind was off the land, the sea smooth and the tides in our favour. George thought that it was much better than banging about the English Channel and at once became an ardent admirer of the East Coast and its bewitching sands.

Freddie was all in favour of the Estuary, too, even though (so I discovered later) his ideas on the shape and size of the British Isles were very hazy. It was the smoothness of the water and the resultant absence of sea-sickness which affected his judgement.

By this time our new hands were settling down to ship board life. They got used to scrubbing decks, setting sails and heaving on winch and windlass handles. They did not have a very high opinion of each other but both, in spite of vastly divergent trains of thought, became useful members of our little company. And while Harry kept a watchful eye on their work I had to exercise a degree of tact to keep their contrasting views from coming into open conflict. For it cannot be said that a gentleman of the Indian Army and a gentleman of Wormwood Scrubs are the best of bedfellows.

But hardship is a great leveller and a gale of wind in the North Sea soon blows away any differences of opinion. That is what we got that night.

It was dark when we rounded Orfordness and the breeze had backed to the southward, accompanied by the evil portent of a downpour of rain. There was a considerable swell rolling up from across the mouth of the Estuary, and I felt a bit anxious when the first few squalls compelled us to lower the head of the topsail.

I did not like the idea of arriving in Yarmouth Roads before daylight and perhaps being compelled to anchor in an exposed position until the tug should come out for us after seven o'clock, which would be the very earliest we might expect her.

I had the mizzen stowed, reefed the mainsail, and ordered the topsail to be clewed in. The flying jib came down next and Harry lashed it down securely.

By midnight the gale was upon us and the strong spring tides that were running helped to kick up a wicked sea in a very short time. No one turned in and Freddie's stomach began to turn out; but I was thankful that George remained in reasonable working condition.

My biggest worry was the prospect of gybing her over in the Stanford Channel, which leads between two shoals into Lowestoft North Road, which in turn takes one into Corton and Yarmouth Roads. I knew that the new gaff the shipyard had given us recently was not much good and the mainsail had really seen its best days. Either, or both, might give way under the heavy jolt of a gybe in such weather.

As bad luck would have it a particularly vicious squall hit us just as we wanted to shape her into the Stanford and the seas were breaking over our quarter in a somewhat alarming manner. To have gybed her then would have been to court disaster on one of the shoals, so, with two of us at the wheel, we had to let her run on outside the Holm and Corton sands until we could see the dim glow of the Corton lightship. All coastwise lights had been dimmed to a visibility of one mile on the outbreak of war.

It was my intention, having more sea room here than in the narrow Stanford Channel, to watch for a chance to gybe her over and stretch in through the Hewett Channel. We could then anchor between the high part of the Scroby Sands, which would form a bit of a breakwater, and the northern part of Yarmouth town. The flood tide had started and would help to check the barge into the land once we had brought the wind on to the port quarter.

Had the tide not been running hard to the southward I would have sailed her right between the pier-heads and into the harbour. But I have previously given the reader a rough idea of the difficulties of making this entrance on a spring flood, and the risk was not justifiable on such a dark and stormy night, especially as the pier-head lights might have been extinguished altogether for all I knew.

An error of judgement close to the piers would not only have resulted in the loss of the *Martinet* but the crew would have had a poor chance of getting ashore alive. So I prayed for a lull and for a smooth patch to get this all-important gybe accomplished.

All hands mustered aft by the wheelhouse. Even Freddie, who knew absolutely nothing about the arts of sailing, realised that this was a tense moment and that his life was perhaps in danger if something should go wrong.

While we hung on, waiting for the critical moment when the spars and canvas should be sent flying from one side to the other, a breaking sea crashed aboard on the lee quarter, carrying away the lifeboat, pulling down the davits and filling the decks up to the level of the top of the bulwarks.

For a moment practically the whole ship was under water. I was standing in about four feet of rushing water at the wheel and almost washed off my feet. The rest clung to various parts of the wheelhouse except George, who was carried across the deck but managed to grab the mizzen rigging and save himself from going overside.

Sluggishly she rose and the water cascaded from her scuppers. George picked himself up and asked me if I thought it was necessary to put life-jackets on.

I said 'Yes, if you'd feel more comfortable with one on.'

So Harry went below and fetched them up and all three laced them on. That last sea had shaken even the mate's confidence a bit. He brought a life-jacket for me, but I'm rather prejudiced against them. I always reckon that if you're going to stick to the ship (and we had no option, especially with the lifeboat gone) such things only hamper a man's movements.

Also, if you were washed overboard in such weather you would be sure to drown. And if I've got to drown I don't want to be cluttered up with one of these things. Salvation lay with the ship, not with a lifebelt. If the ship foundered, so would we. So my intuition was to keep myself free and unhampered to do battle with the black, wooden shape to which we trusted our lives all the year round.

I believed that all would be well in the end and I think it was only the bad reputation of the wicked old *Martinet* that cast a shadow of doubt over my mind.

Another sea ran over us, washed clear, and then there was a

smooth patch. I knew that our time had come.

'Stand by. Gybe-oh!'

For a moment the main boom hesitated threateningly over the rail. Then over she came with a crash. There was a rending of canvas, a snapping and splintering of timber aloft, and the ship gave a violent lurch to starboard.

'What's happened?' yelled Harry.

It was so dark we could not see half the length of the deck. But I knew at once what the trouble was. The main gaff had broken and the mainsail had gone to pieces.

The seas broke over us continuously, for the lack of canvas made her roll terribly. Often she dipped her weather rail right into an on-coming sea. I was worried that a wedge might come out and the hatch cloths start to lift, but it was not safe to send a man along the midship decks to find out. We just had to take that chance.

I felt an inward thankfulness that we had entered the Hewetts Channel while the spring flood was running at its hardest, for otherwise we should have most surely been wrecked on the Scroby Sands that night. But the tide held us clear of the shoal water while the head sail drew the ship in towards the land and into smoother water.

There was not a hope of doing anything about the broken gaff and the remains of the mainsail. Together they flogged and thundered round the mast and rigging but could not do any serious harm. The only trouble was that a broken piece of the spar cut the topsail adrift from its gasket so that it flogged round the cross-trees and blew to ribbons in a matter of a few seconds. But that seemed a mere fleabite compared with all else that had happened.

Presently I could make out the St. Nicholas lightship, and the clattering of our shreds of canvas brought a hail from the lightship men.

'Are you all right?' they shouted.

'We're all right,' I bawled back. 'Going to bring up in the roads.'

They could have sent a signal to the shore if we had required any assistance.

We were safe when we got between the Nicholas and the shore, and the seas were not so dangerous. As we ran a little further northward the water became fit to anchor and we let go forty-five fathoms of chain. The anchor bit well in and held. Although she pitched heavily for a time it seemed like Heaven after the belting we had had outside.

We made some attempt to see the extent of the damage. Except that the gaff was in three pieces, the starboard cross-tree bent like a hoop and the whole frapped round with ribbons of canvas, we were not in such bad shape as I had feared. All the hatch wedges were still firmly in the batten hooks and nothing had been washed out of its lashings except the boat. The davits looked a bit drunk and a part of the wheelhouse had disappeared. Also there was a lot of water in the bilges and undoubtedly we had wetted some of the wheat.

But, all things considered, I was far from despondent. The ship was all right. We were all right. Most of the cargo was all right. All we wanted was some new sails, another gaff, a boat, and a cross-tree straightening out.

Thus relieved, I turned in for a couple of hours' sleep. When I awoke the wind had veered off the land and the seas had gone down to something not much bigger than a popple.

After we had breakfasted the old paddle tug *United Services* came out to tow us into the harbour. She was quite an antique, being sixty-eight years old and clench built (that is with overlapping planks like a rowing boat). I think she was the last paddle tug in service in the British Isles and by a coincidence the *Martinet,* the last of the boomies, was the last barge she ever towed in. The old tug was due to be broken up. She had a crew of three and I think the youngest was sixty-eight.

So that particular morning was quite a memorable occasion (apart from our overnight adventures), as she paddled her way up the long, narrow haven with a battered old sailing vessel in tow, though I do not suppose a single one of the folk who stared at us from the shore realised it.

From Yarmouth there is a long, wearisome tow up the River Yare to Norwich. It generally takes about six hours, sometimes more. There is very little water and often our bottom was sliding over the mud, churning up a dirty, smelly wake astern and making steering an arduous and arm-aching job.

The scenery is artistic, the windmills picturesque, the riverside villages a delight to look upon—but it needs more than that to counterbalance the sharp bends to be negotiated, the narrow bridge-holes to be shot and, worst of all, that wretched railway bridge at Norwich. This last bridge never seems to open until:

(1) those aboard the vessel wishing to go through have shouted themselves hoarse and broken the foghorn with repeated and vicious blasts;

(2) the tug skipper has blown all the steam he can spare on his whistle;

(3) all concerned have come to the end of their vocabulary of evil words (not to mention caustic opinions on the railway in general) and many terrible oaths directed at the men whose duty it is to let the water-borne traffic through between trains.

After about an hour of this hullabaloo a railwayman strolled out of his cosy hut and, very leisurely, swung open the bridge.

Once the skipper of a barge, the *Hydrogen* I believe her name was, sustained a ghastly injury to his arm while towing up to Norwich, and the only thing to be done was to get him to Norwich hospital as quickly as possible. The old tug skipper has more than once told me the story of how his driver (engineer) ran the engines as they had never been run before and the whistle was kept screeching long before the bridge was sighted. The master of the tug yelled and shouted to the railwaymen to open the bridge. But he was expecting too much.

He was made to tie up and wait for over an hour, and when at last they condescended to let him through he gave them his honest opinion. (I cannot repeat that part of his story in full, though it is most instructive and illuminating.)

'You ought to be ashamed of yourselves,' he said. 'That man is lying there in agony.'

A dull flabby face looked over the rails.

'Well I can't help it if he is.'

By this time the tug was through, but the mate of the barge following was able to sum up the situation in a few crisp sentences.

The men on the Norwich railway bridge are not very popular with the men who work on the river. Probably the reader will have surmised that much by now for himself.

•••••

We were a sad ship in Norwich. Not because of our unfortunate passage or the damage to our gear. Harry had made his last trip as mate of the *Martinet* and was leaving us to sign on a motor-coaster named the *Annuity*. She was the company's smallest motor ship but, by going into power, Harry had set himself on the road to a good job.

He was wise in making the change, I knew, but we had worked and sailed together for over two years and his departure seemed quite a blow.

A telegram came for him with orders to proceed to London by train to join his new ship, and we saw him off at the station on the day after our arrival in Norwich.

He had two main reasons for going into a power-driven vessel. Firstly, the wages were better and more regular, and this was especially welcome since he had taken on extra financial responsibilities at home, owing to his father's illness. Secondly, he wanted to get on in a seafaring career and could see that sailing ships were but glories of the past, outmoded and obsolete. (I knew that, too, but was stupidly reluctant to admit it.)

Several years later Harry came to see me on one of his periodical visits and gleefully produced from his pocket a second mate's deep-sea certificate. He now walks the bridge of a big steamer of some eight thousand tons, and I have been told that he is a highly efficient officer.

He often tells me that his experience in the sailing barges always kept him a step ahead of steam-trained officers in any tasks where vigilance, smart seamanship and initiative were required.

By his dexterous helmsmanship he once brought a big ship out of a dangerous situation in a terrific winter gale off the southern coast of Ireland. He confided to me that he got her clear of the land by handling her like a sailing vessel and she was the only ship of the convoy to be in her proper station when the weather became fine.

On another occasion he was torpedoed off East Africa and took charge of a lifeboat full of survivors. He sailed her some two hundred miles to land, being the only man in the boat who had a practical knowledge of sailing.

And now, as we grow a little grey, he drops in to see me at my house when he is home from his distant voyages. We talk of topsails and leeboards, of wettings down-Channel and of those impromptu, hell-for-leather races we used to have against other barges.

'They laugh at me aboard now,' he will say, 'when I tell them that I was once a sailing bargeman. Look down their noses and sneer. But they don't know, do they? They don't know.'

And he wags his head, puffs his pipe, and settles down again to reminiscence.

'Do you remember that time off the north-east Gunfleet —'

• • • • •

The new mate was of a very different stamp. Compared with Harry's high standard he was a very poor substitute. Hard working at things he liked doing and lazy at anything else. I could see that he did not intend to stay with us for very long.

The owners arranged for us to be towed back to London and who should arrive in Yarmouth to do the job but Harry's *Annuity.* We were caught in a south-westerly gale on the way back and had a lively night dragging anchors in Hollesley Bay. The *Annuity* anchored ahead of us at first and when the gale came on about midnight I remember her driving stern first past the *Martinet,* as though she was under way and going full speed astern. She hove up her anchor, steamed back into position, and let go again. Within an hour she was dragging by us again. Once more she weighed and steamed up ahead and let go afresh.

This little cycle of events went on all night. Whenever I looked up on deck the *Annuity* was either dragging astern as though she had no anchor or else steaming back to where she came from. Harry told me afterwards that sixty fathoms of chain were paid out each time, but her stockless patent anchor could not get a grip.

The *Martinet* steadily dragged fifty fathoms from abreast of Orford Haven down past Orford Ness, and her anchor eventually picked up a telegraph cable. This held her until daylight but we had a nice old job getting clear of it. We had to lift the cable up off the bottom of the sea and sling it with our big towing wire before we could slack the anchor clear.

We got a beautiful new mainsail at Greenhithe. The sailmaker there will never make a better sail and it stretched to a perfect fit. A new topsail was made to go over it and we had a quick overhaul of all our running and standing gear.

Soon there was a cargo of cotton seed for Southampton to be loaded in the Millwall Dock. Cotton seed is very light stuff and we trimmed under her decks until we were nearly choked. We managed to get one hundred and thirty-eight tons into her, but for three days after that I could only speak in a whisper. The shreds of cotton from the seed had stuck in my throat. If I wanted the mate to let go the anchor I either had to make signs or run forward and whisper in his ear.

It was while we were lying alongside the discharging berth in Southampton, up the Itchen River by Northam Bridge, that I slipped on a ladder while going aboard in the dark. Although I did not fall right down into the water, grabbing one of the lower

rungs in my descent, I was for a moment suspended between the
Martinet's tarry hull and the wooden quay. It seemed that such a
chance was too much for the *Martinet's* wicked spirit to miss. At
that very moment she closed into the quay to crush me to pulp on
the wall; but with one of those frantic efforts which one makes in
such circumstances, I pulled my body up above the level of the
deck so that only my boots were jammed in between the
bulwarks and the quay as she came to.

I suppose that her movement was really caused by a flush of
fresh water from under Northam Bridge, but it did seem that
what the old sailors said about her was true. 'She'll kill you if she
gets the chance.' All that night their words rang in my ears and I
believe that for once superstition began to get the better of me. It
took several pints the next morning to laugh it off.

We were about three weeks on the round trip because we
were held up for several days in Ryde Roads with a strong
easterly wind. But as the cotton seed had been at the rate of
seventeen-and-six a ton, which was reckoned pretty good in
those days, we were well satisfied with the proceeds.

There was another job for us when we got back, to load wheat
for Norwich in the Millwall Dock. It was then, just as we were
loaded and ready for sea, that the mate left the ship at an hour's
notice.

• • • • •

There were a lot of crew changes in the *Martinet* about this
time. While we were re-fitting at Greenhithe, George Vlasto had
gone off to join the Navy, having completed his necessary sea-
time with us. I was sorry to see him off as he had been an
excellent and entertaining companion, a willing worker, a splendid
dart-player (winning us many an unpaid pint) and had never
grumbled at hardship. In fact, he had lived up to all the good
recommendations that old Colombos had given him at Poole
nearly three months before.

Freddie left too. He went off as cook of a motor ship in the
same firm and by all accounts regaled the forecastle hands with
lurid tales of his 'time in sail'. He sailed away to Hull, and I
never expected to see him again unless it was by accident. But I

was wrong. A year later he swung his legs over the *Martinet's* rail as she lay in the Albert Dock, announced that he was fed up with motor and steam ships, and wanted his old job back. I had nothing against him, for he had always been a trier, and, as there happened to be a vacancy, I was once more able to watch him cheat at cards, swindle the dockees, outflank the police, and hear his tales of the travelling fairs in which he had spent most of his life.

Freddie used to enrage most people by his talk and his manners, and many a man I know has sworn to do him injury. But in his dealings with me he was always straight and honourable. If I gave him money to buy stores he would account for it to the very last halfpenny. If I asked him to go ashore and get me some tobacco when we lay in out-of-the-way anchorages he would always get it, even if it meant miles of walking through rain or snow. In fact, he would rush to do me a favour at the slightest suggestion on my part.

I put this faithful, dog-like service down to his inherent cunning, he having decided that the skipper was the one to keep in with and that all the rest, ashore and afloat, were just a lot of mugs.

Just before the new mate cleared out at Millwall there came aboard a sturdy fellow in his thirties, who had been recommended to me by a friend ashore. This new arrival was keen to go to sea in a barge and was by no means a newcomer to salt water. He had sailed in a yacht to Spain and the Baltic, as well as coastal trips, and had a rough idea about barges from a passage he had made in the *Mayflower* from Maldon.

He signed on as fourth hand at first, his idea being to become familiar with the everyday work before trying to get a berth as mate in a small barge. His name was Jerry Thomason.

Old Alf Fielder, skipper of the *Her Majesty*, used to say that all you could expect of a barge hand these days was that he be 'strong and civil'. Thomason filled the bill in this respect and exceeded these modest qualifications by being a student of all sailing vessels and a tireless worker at even the most uncongenial tasks.

Although he had had a classical education at Clifton and Cambridge, he would vigorously scrub out the lavatory, scrape the topmast, peel potatoes and take a trick at the wheel as all part

of the day's work. Although he was rather too old to start
learning about barges I could see that he had the makings of a
first class seaman. That he lacked experience of coastal and river
trading was obvious, and consequently he lacked confidence as
well. But when the mate departed at such short notice I gambled
on Jerry's inexperience and he blossomed out overnight as mate
of the *Martinet*. It was a gamble that I never regretted.

He assured me that he was not good enough to be mate, but I
told him that it was too late to get anyone else and that he would
just have to get on with it. The mate had cleared out at nine
o'clock in the evening and we had to be out of the dock at four in
the morning. He promised to do his best and in the small, dark
hours of a February morn we scrambled through the lock and
sailed away down Limehouse Reach.

There were a hundred-and-one things I had to show him and
explain to him on the way, but it is no great trouble to do that
with one who is ready and anxious to learn. By the time we got to
Norwich (it was one of those uneventful passages) he was
beginning to shape very well.

We had with us as third hand a peculiar product of the street
corners—a pale-faced, ill-nourished, fag-smoking lad from
Lambeth. This youngster, when he first joined the ship as a
greenhorn, did not even know how to eat a hot dinner. On his
first day he sat down in the cabin to a well-filled platter of roast
beef, vegetables and duff. He would not eat it.

He said he was not used to those sort of meals and would
rather have a tin of beans or some fish and chips. In fact, he
would not even sit down at the table. Rather than that, he would
roam about or lean against the door-post munching bits of this
and that until such times as we were able to educate him to eat a
proper meal off a table. It took several weeks and many an angry
word to make him do it, but once it was accomplished he
changed visibly from day to day. The open-air life and good food
soon took the pallor from his cheeks and put flesh on to his
miserable body.

I have often had to teach young beginners the business of
seafaring but never before or since have I had to educate a lad on
how to fill his stomach.

Of course, third hands don't last very long aboard a barge and we used to collect and dispose of quite a variety of strange specimens. Harry used to say that we used them up and threw them away as required. Generally they stayed long enough to learn how to handle a boat in a tideway, set sails and make ropes fast properly. Then they would get a job as mate of a small barge—that is, if they didn't sicken of the life and go back to the shore.

Chapter Fourteen

THE CRASH AND VIOLENCE OF WAR DESCENDED about the *Martinet* with rather alarming suddenness.

We were sailing peacefully down the East Swin on our way to Yarmouth with a cargo of rice. It was a lovely day, the sun softening the pitch in the decks and a light breeze taking us slowly but very pleasantly towards our destination.

I was literally lounging at the wheel; the mate was sprawled on the main hatches, recumbent and semiconscious; and the new cook was meditating over our little white bow wave. We had had an excellent dinner and an air of dreamy satisfaction seemed to pervade the whole ship.

The war had been on for nearly a year and had hardly affected either us or our work. I had become used to the nuisance of the Naval Control and had learned how and when to circumvent or disregard the majority of their unwelcome instructions. I had also found that terrific bouts of swearing at naval patrols and examination boats were rather a waste of breath.

Some of their boats were manned by ex-bank clerks, barbers, grocers and the rakings of the offices and counters of the metropolis. A number were so ignorant in a seafaring sense that it paid to answer their questions and orders with a plain 'yes' or 'no'—and then go on our way and take no more notice of what they had said. But on this particular day, in the August of 1940, the war came upon us in reality.

There was a steady droning sound from the south-east which grew louder and louder until it became a veritable roar. The mate sat up and listened. Then the cook came running aft.

'Those are aeroplanes, skipper,' the boy said excitedly, 'there must be hundreds of them.'

We scanned the sunlit sky and there they were almost above us—a great mass of silvery planes heading for the Essex shore.

'They must be Germans,' said the mate. 'We wouldn't have all those bombers out together.'

He was right. He and the cook started counting them—sixty-eight in all they made it. I began to wonder what we had better do. We were the only vessel in sight and there were all those bombers over our heads with six or seven bombs apiece—one of which would be quite sufficient, if well aimed, to cause the sudden disintegration and disappearance of the *Martinet* and her crew.

I ordered the lashings to be taken off the lifeboat and some food and water put in her. Then I went below and put my wallet and ship's papers in my pocket.

I came on deck again just in time to see a thrilling sight—and one which I shall never forget.

From the direction of the North Foreland came three tiny dots—British fighters flying at a great pace straight for the rear of that formidable mass of planes. For sheer courage and audacity those three pilots exceeded anything I have ever known or seen. I had not realised that there were young men in England who could be so recklessly brave. They flew right in amongst the mass formation of bombers and the vicious rattle of machine-guns filled the air.

A number of German fighters, which we had not noticed before, swooped down from high above the battle to ward off the attackers, but the three British pilots seemed to disregard them and closed with the big bombers.

Things happened too quickly for me to keep track of the fight. There was a series of whistling sounds (which were to be all too familiar to British ears in the desperate months to come) and seven bombs exploded in a line about two hundred yards off our port beam.

Whether or not they were intended for the *Martinet* we shall never know. More likely, I think, that they were let go by a damaged plane. But it made the old ship shake like a leaf.

For several minutes after the last one had exploded the barge continued to vibrate violently and we discovered later that a 'cement box' which had been put in her counter between the timbers to stop a leak had fallen to pieces.

A black aeroplane with German markings came gently spiralling down and then finished up with a sudden header and a great splash into the Barrow Deeps. Not far from us a parachute drifted very slowly and I could plainly see the German suspended beneath it. He fell into the water just off our starboard quarter.

I conducted a rapid argument with myself as to what I should do about him.

'If he didn't want to drown or get killed he shouldn't have come here,' I said to myself. 'This isn't his country. And he's only come here to try and kill people with his bombs.'

This was one of the Germans who threatened to lay Britain's cities in ashes. That meant that they would bomb and kill women and children and smash up people's homes. Not long before I had myself been married to a fair maid of Kent; and this German in the water might well have been on his way to kill or maim her and smash up our little home. I watched the parachute settle over the top of him as he hit the water and I could see him struggling beneath it.

The killer had provided his own shroud. In its folds he disappeared. I was glad; it served him right.

The sky-fight above had moved away from us and I could see bombs exploding on shore. I thought of everyday people being slaughtered in their own homes and I felt very angry. I knew that in those brief and exciting moments I had been shaken out of my old peaceful and contented life and became, as folk on shore had become, just another very determined Englishman—determined not to bow my head to these brutal and arrogant Germans.

The next day, as the Yarmouth tug towed us up the haven, the air-raid sirens were wailing and I could hear gunfire in the distance. The war had come home to us at last. No longer was it the concern only of men trained to arms, but the business of each and every one of us. The barbarians were at the gate.

While I was ashore in Yarmouth I met a small boy standing outside an air-raid shelter. The mate and I were hanging about in the vicinity of the shelter too, because there was a scrap going on in the clouds overhead. When the lad spoke I knew he was a cockney and asked him if he was having a holiday. Yarmouth is a favourite resort for Londoners.

'No,' he replied, 'my Mum sent me down here to stay wiv me aunt. London's all in bits.'

His childish description of the heavy air-raids which the Germans had started to make on London led me to question him more closely, for my home was only fourteen miles outside the capital—at a village called Bexley in Kent.

It was tragic to hear him talk, in his innocent little piping voice, of the terrors which had visited the district where he lived. Mrs. So-and-So had been killed in the grocer's shop; the house next door was knocked down; something had evidently happened to his father coming home from work but they had not told him what; the streets were all littered with glass ——— .

That afternoon, with a heart full of anxiety, I boarded a train for London. It crawled into Liverpool Street Station about ten o'clock at night.

As I came out of the station I saw policemen in steel helmets. The streets were dark and deserted. I walked swiftly down Gracechurch Street to get to London Bridge Station. Away to the eastward I could see the fierce red glow of gigantic fires, the flames of some shooting up high above the roof-top horizon. Guns of all calibres were barking and roaring.

Near the Monument I got my first sight of the work of the barbarians. A bank which I used to use was a smoking heap of rubble. The familiar corner of King William Street was blasted out of shape. The roadway was thick with bricks and broken glass. An uprooted lamp-post lay across the pavement. There was blood, too, dark and congealed. I could smell it.

I was glad I hadn't picked that German airman out of the water. Had I seen this first I should probably have shot him.

I picked my way over the mess and ran across London Bridge. There was a bomber coming up the river and I had no desire to be caught on the bridge. I felt bitterly angry and wished I had hands and arms long enough to claw him down and beat his brains out.

At London Bridge Station there was more rubble, more devastation, more smoking ruins. I asked two policemen if there was any chance of getting a loop-line train and they laughed.

'Gawd blimey, sailor, there ain't been no trains out of here for a week.'

A youngster in the uniform of the R.A.F. who came along after me was given similar information. I overheard him say that he wanted to get to Sidcup, and in a few minutes we had struck up a rough acquaintanceship and held a council of war. What were we going to do? His destination was not far from mine.

Walk. That was the only solution. The policemen thought it was the best thing we could do. They advised us to be careful in the Old Kent Road district as things were very bad down there.

So, each glad of the other's company, we set off on our trek through the south-eastern suburbs. Planes droned overhead to be welcomed by the din of the anti-aircraft guns. Bombs fell; shrapnel whistled and pattered around us; fresh fires sprang up in people's houses and shops. Through all this we trudged resolutely.

Sometimes we passed crowds of people dragging men and women from out of smouldering heaps of brick and ashes. We stopped once or twice to see if our help was needed, but generally there were plenty on the job already. So we walked on, mile after mile, between rows of furniture stacked on the pavements and the pitiful little bundles of poor people's treasures.

I lost my companion at Lewisham. A crowded Army lorry came careering down the street, swerving wildly round the bomb craters and piles of rubble. The airman signalled for a lift.

'We can take one,' the soldiers shouted as they pulled up.

'Go on,' I urged the airman, 'chaps in your concern are wanted by the look of things.'

And so I completed the journey alone. When I reached my house the guns on Dartford Heath were banging like hell let loose and those on neighbouring sites seemed to be competing with each other as to who could send up the most shells in the shortest time. This was one of the outer defence lines of London.

I found my house intact and my wife sleeping, or trying to sleep, under the stairs. Some neighbours were stretched out in the passage. But I was home; and everything was all right. Bombs, guns, shrapnel and sore feet were, as far as was possible, put out of mind.

My house was damaged one morning while I was at home. A Spitfire fighter machine was shot down by a German in a fight overhead and parts of the British plane's engine came to rest in our attic, in the front room and on the stairs. While repairs were being carried out I took my wife back to Yarmouth and on board the *Martinet.* The old ship's beams and timbers seemed very safe and friendly after the wracking hell of London.

The presence of my wife on board had a very marked effect upon the ship and her crew. The cabin was transformed into a little palace. The mate shaved every day, or nearly every day, and the cook used to wash his hands before making the duff The language used on board was crisp, plain and polite. Displeasure could be shown only by a gesture of impatience or a sigh.

The wharf foreman, who had the reputation of wanting us to be continually shifting the ship a bit ahead or astern to facilitate his work, wouldn't trouble us for the worlds and each morning brought bunches of flowers from his garden for the cabin.

The men in the hold hardly spoke a word. They 'dussn't', as people say in Norfolk. They just got on with humping the sacks of rice about and did not, to my knowledge, pass a single audible comment on the way it had been stowed. And all these things, as every bargeman knows, are well nigh unbelievable.

I had urgent orders to get to Rochester and load a cargo of coke for Margate. There was a shortage of craft in Rochester and a shortage of coke in Margate. We sailed away with a westerly wind and there was a nasty swell out in the roads. A motor torpedo-boat was patrolling off Corton and her lieutenant-in-charge spotted my wife sitting on the cabin skylight. He brought his vessel close and gave us a hail.

'Good morning, skipper,' he shouted politely, 'it's rather unusual to have ladies aboard in war time, isn't it?'

I was about to answer 'that's not a lady, that's my old woman'; but I had not been married long enough to take a liberty like that. So I told him that she was signed on as one of the crew.

'All right,' he said, 'I'll escort you a little way.'

And so the old *Martinet,* floundering along against a head wind, was duly accompanied for about an hour by this white and

gleaming little motor vessel with the white ensign fluttering at
her stern. It is the only occasion on which I have had the immediate
and personal protection of one of His Majesty's ships. We all felt
honoured.

My wife rather ruined the effect of all this by being heartily
sick to leeward, taking care in doing so to keep out of sight of the
lieutenant. He left us near Lowestoft and we plugged along until
the tide was done and had to anchor off Aldeburgh. The next
night we had to lie under the lee of the Gunfleet sands—for we
were not allowed to sail in the hours of darkness for fear of a
seaborne invasion by the Germans, who had by then possessed
themselves of the whole of the Continental coastline. The French
had surrendered in June and the British Expeditionary Force was
thrown out via Dunkirk. Many fine sailing barges were lost on
the beaches there in getting the men back to England. The *Ethel
Everard,* the *Aidie* and *the Barbara Jean*—three of the finest
coasting sailormen trading out of London—had to be left there.
But all that is for someone else to write about, for the affair
would make a dozen books in itself.

The result of this military disaster, so far as we were
concerned, was a series of anti-invasion measures all round the
British coast. Anything under way in the dark within three miles
of the land was liable to be fired upon, so we had to find some
reasonably sheltered anchorage every nightfall. This was not
always possible, especially when breezes were rather uncertain,
and many were the roly-poly nights we had, wondering if we
should be able to get our anchor up in the morning, or perhaps
drag into danger before the dawn.

On this occasion we were lucky, for the weather fell fine and
on the ebb tide the sands uncovered and made a little harbour for
us, even though we were some five or six miles off the land.

The morning was calm and unpromising until, after a few
fickle puffs, a smart northerly breeze sprang up and away went
the *Martinet* like a hare. With the wind abeam and everything set
she was a joy to steer and my wife, who by now had got her sea
legs, was infected by that glorious fascination of sun and sails
and wind. It is a thing a steamboat man never experiences and
never knows. They do miss a lot in those coal and oil
contraptions.

As we approached the Thames boom defences we were met by the usual confusion and delay and the useless pulling up and down of signals imposed upon us by the Naval Control tugs on patrol.

One said we were to hoist a certain signal and proceed to our destination. Then he came back and said we must go to Gravesend for orders before going up the Medway to Rochester. That would have meant losing the cargo of coke.

I felt rather more than annoyed at this and altered course to pass through the Thames gateway of the boom instead of the Medway gateway, which was to the southward. All hands turned to get the sheets in, which was no easy matter in a smart breeze, and between four and five thousand square feet of canvas had to be close-hauled by the three of us. Then the idiot changed his mind again and ordered us to go through the Medway gateway, first reporting to the tug patrolling off there.

Having got the ship into a position to enter the Thames gate it was very difficult to get to the other one without either a heavy gybe with everything set and perhaps doing some damage, or else getting driven on to the boom itself by the strong flood tide. We ran her by the lee—a dangerous thing to do when there is any weight in the wind—and were so busy with our own affairs on deck that I forgot all about the Medway tug and hauled the barge through the gateway at great speed. We left him astern and headed into the river past Sheerness.

Out popped a little motor-boat with some sort of officer aboard. He wanted all particulars of the barge—'where from, where bound, what cargo, master's name, number of crew, any foreigners on board, etc., etc.'

'Why are you not flying the proper signals for entry?' he asked.

I remembered then that we had not reported to the Medway gate tug and thought up a quick lie to avoid any further delays and difficulties. I was more anxious to get to Rochester and load that coke than to conform to their fiddling regulations, and the tide had already flowed for nearly three hours. Time was getting short.

'We hauled them down again after we were inside the boom,' I shouted.

That seemed to satisfy him and we went on, threading our

way through the crowd of minesweepers and destroyers which lay
to the moorings in the river. I thanked my lucky stars that we had
not been forced to take a pilot, as we had been in the *Northdown.*

Off Chatham the wind headed us and it became a ticklish
business to get the barge to windward in the narrow and crowded
parts of the river. Just as we were making a delicate manoeuvre
between some moored ships, another motor-boat shot out from the
shore and threw a hook into our mizzen rigging, the officer asking
the same rigmarole of questions which we had been through twice
already.

The drag of the motor-boat on our lee quarter canted the
barge's head off the wind so that she would not come about and we
nearly hit a destroyer which was coming down the river. I had to
stand the *Martinet* over into shallow water, heave the leeboards up,
and box her round with the mizzen and headsails with her bottom
only a foot clear of the mud.

This caused my only lapse during my wife's stay on board.
Forgetting her presence on deck I called the motor-boat officer all
the names I could lay my tongue to and told him what I thought of
Navy sailors in general. My wife fled into the galley and shut the
door until I had finished and the mate chopped through the
offending hook-rope and cast the motor-boat adrift. We should
have gone ashore if he hadn't.

In spite of all this we got to Rochester just in time and the
crews of the other barges, knowing we were late, swarmed
aboard to lend us a hand. There was old Cully, skipper of the
Cambria, Frank Day and his son Albert from the *Martha,* Harry
Delaney of the *Britisher* and several old mates and third hands.
While we sat down to dinner they berthed the *Martinet,* stowed
the sails up, got the hatches and beams off, and started the
loading. By tea-time the barge was loaded and hauled off to the
buoy. All things considered, this was not a bad achievement in
face of the Naval Control.

The next morning we had a visit from above in the form of a
stick of bombs dropped by a German Heinkel plane. One fell in
the river between the barges and the wharf and my impression
was that all the craft lifted out of the water a couple of feet, gave
a sudden convulsion, and then settled down again, none the worse.
The rest of the bombs spent their energies blowing up clouds of

mud on some nearby marshes. My wife went home again from Rochester (our house having been repaired) and when we sailed for Margate her civilising influence fell away from us all too rapidly. Before long the flowers in the cabin had faded and died, the mate was going about with five days' growth on his chin, and the cook had returned to his old habit of singing in the lavatory.

When we were off Margate Hook Sand an easterly gale came hustling up the Estuary and we had to lie there at anchor and ride it out for two days and two nights. This was no great hardship, although it was too rough for us to attempt to heave the anchor up. We gave her about forty fathoms of chain, kept a strict watch on the pumps, and for the rest of the time ate, slept, and played cards.

When at last the wind veered off the land we set the sails and within an hour of our getting under way the Margate huffler was clambering over the quarter boards. With the aid of his motor-boat he shot the barge round the little stone breakwater which forms the harbour and berthed her astern of the *Martha*. All the other barges had sailed ahead of us and just missed the easterly breeze. The *Cambria* and the *Britisher* were already empty, and the *Martha* had only a few hours' work left in her.

I made a dash home on the train to see if our house was still there. I eventually got used to that awful feeling of uncertainty on my visits home as I walked up our road, wondering whether I was going to find the place intact or just a heap of rubble.

The Margate job done, we returned to London light and fell upon bad times again. The docks and wharves of London River were being battered and burnt in the air-raids and the big foreign-going ships, which usually provided the bulk of our cargoes, almost ceased to use the port. They discharged further north in safer areas.

For six weeks the *Martinet* swung to her anchor off Greenhithe. Money was running short and the raids got worse. Every day I left home and went to the office. Every day the clerk shook his head. 'Nothing for you to-day, skipper.'

Thirty-six times he said that and I reached a condition of financial strain when the bus fare became a burden and I had to make the journey of seven miles each way on an old bicycle.

The 'Governor' did his best to get us a freight, but time and again the cargoes he hoped for did not materialise. Then at last the great day came.

'You are wanted at Number Seven Shed in the King George Dock to load linseed for Ipswich.'

We were aboard and under way almost before the words were out of his mouth. The cook had left us but that did not matter. Jerry and I hove that anchor up and set the sails with the strength and energy of a dozen men. The *Martinet* was in the dock that night and we hove her through the basin while the guns blazed away at the bombers overhead. I prayed that they wouldn't drop one on Number Seven Shed.

We had to wait several days to get loaded. During this time I cast about for a third hand of some sort. I was willing to take on anyone from a half-wit to a duke, so long as he could heave on ropes and turn a winch handle round. Then who should come on board one morning but the worthy Freddie, our ex-roundabout man from Poole. He wanted to ship with me again and I signed him on straight away.

As if to celebrate his arrival we had a special blitz on the dock that night. Flares fell on the quays and illuminated the place like daylight. To add to this unwanted illumination a big fire got going over at Beckton, which is just outside the dock area.

The *Martinet* jumped and trembled as high explosives fell upon the warehouses and in the water. Bits of quayside, broken bricks and shrapnel littered her decks. Every now and then we had to retreat to a nearby air-raid shelter. But the barge escaped damage and Number Seven Shed was not hit.

We got our cargo and cleared out of the dock as quickly as possible. Two days later we were berthed in the cut at Ipswich, having had a beautiful south-west wind to take us all the way there from London.

Back in London work fell off again but eventually we got another cargo for Ipswich. These two freights were all we earned between October and Christmas—about three pounds a week for me and thirty bob for the mate.

It was not a good winter for a newly-married man, although by some womanly miracle my wife got together a comfortable home. In spite of the raids and our lack of money she made the place look as though she had married—not the skipper of the old *Martinet*—but some wealthy financier, or even a ship-owner.

Chapter Fifteen

JUST BEFORE CHRISTMAS the *Martinet* and the *Martha* were sent to Greenwich Buoys to load fertiliser for Ipswich. This freight was a godsend as it saved me from a stoney-broke Yuletide.

The boomie loaded first and, after collecting a good fat sub, we took advantage of the light south-westerly airs to run away down to the Yantlet. The weather was very fine for the time of year and the next day it took us nearly all the ebb tide to sail down the West Swin. But the time did not lag, for this fertiliser was very heavy stuff and all the weight was in the bottom half of the ship. As a result we were on the pumps almost continuously. Whether it was the type of cargo, the shaking she had had from the bombs or badly-done repairs I am not sure; but she leaked abominably. As soon as the pump sucked and the hands had had a rest and smoke they had to go at it again. Squeak, squeak, squeak went the long iron handle, all the way from Southend to the Gunfleet Lighthouse, where we anchored for the night.

We were drawing nine feet six inches and there was very little water over the Spitway owing to the poor tides. So we decided to sail 'down round'—that is, via the North-East Gunfleet buoy. As we lay off the lighthouse that night the sea had almost a glassy smoothness. Only a gentle swell gave her a slight rolling motion. We hoped that this fine weather would mean that, with the ship lying quietly to her cable, we should have a spell off from the pumps.

The mate sucked her out and we had our evening meal. By the time we had finished we could hear water slopping about in the well and once more we had to turn to. In the end, each man had to work two-hour watches at the pump all through the night. And nothing breaks a sailorman's heart quicker than a pump that does not suck. We were thankful for the first streaks of daylight so that we could get under way and run her into Harwich.

It was a busy day for us as we reached up the Orwell, one man steering and tending the lee-boards and another looking after the sheets and halliards, and the third grinding his heart out on the pump. Whoever had a minute to spare gave an eye to the cooking.

We berthed at Cliff Quay, which is just outside Ipswich Dock, that afternoon and kept ourselves amused with the pump until the crane started getting the cargo out in the morning. It looked a bit soggy in parts and I imagined what an awful muck it would have been if we had for one moment neglected the pumps.

A shipwright was supposed to have caulked the bad places in her hull a week or two previously—but then, shipwrights don't have to go to sea, and they don't have to pump. Nor do some of them lose any sleep at the thought of some poor sailorman pumping for dear life from dusk till dawn on a winter's night.

In these days, when skilled craftsmanship is on the decline, a thorough and conscientious shipwright is a prize indeed. There are some splendid craftsmen to be found in the barge yards round the Thames Estuary and East Coast. There are also to be found some of the most useless and lazy articles of humanity I have ever had to suffer from.

Just after we had finished discharging, Frank Day arrived in the *Martha*. He brought with him a tragic tale of disasters in the waters just below Southend. Within about three days a dozen or more ships, mostly small motor and steam coasters, had been blown up by a new sort of mine dropped from German aeroplanes. This was not the magnetic type, which had already sent several steamers to the bottom of the Estuary, but a thing called an acoustic mine, which was exploded by the vibration of the ship. Of course, this mine could be used only in fairly shallow water, but no doubt the Germans hoped to make our ports too dangerous for ships to use by sowing them thickly in the approaches.

Some of our own company's ships had gone and the names of sailors we knew, many of them ex-bargemen, were among those who had lost their lives. In days that followed all of us men on the coast became accustomed to hearing of ships and shipmates being blown to pieces almost every day. You would see a seaman having a quiet pint in a waterside pub one day and the next be told that he was drowned or killed. It was almost unbelievable at first but we got used to the idea when the truth of it was thrust upon us.

We moored up the *Martinet* and the *Martha* for Christmas (there being no orders for either of us) and went home. In the train we talked about the new mine and wondered whether it would blow up sailing barges.

• • • • •

They were dark days in the winter of 1940—41. They were dark for anyone who lived in England at that time. No amount of retribution and repentance will ever wipe out the medieval barbarism of the Germans at that period. Their bombs crashed down without aim or purpose other than to destroy, to kill, and to terrify. The fact that they were eventually repaid in their own kind still does not clean the slate, even though they squealed and whined despicably when the British started to bomb them back in earnest.

I felt particularly angry about this outrageous slaughter of ordinarily peaceful folk in their own homes, because my own home was soon to be occupied by a completely innocent and helpless little person. There was a baby on the way.

Many a father can think back, and sometimes laugh, about the state he worried himself into before the arrival of his firstborn in times when all was peace and safety. There is no need for me to describe how I felt with the German air blitz at its height and with the value of human life reduced to a minimum.

On top of all this, trade was in a bad way and I was getting desperately short of money. Like most fathers-to-be, I wanted to give my wife at least half the world and all the comforts in it. But you can't do that on fourpence.

All this leads up to a remarkable passage we made to Norwich in atrocious weather with a cargo of bulk wheat from London. This cargo was a most profitable affair compared with anything we had done so far. I was offered a pound a ton and there were 198 ½ tons to be loaded. I reckoned up my share of the proceeds and calculated that if the trip was made in reasonably quick time I should be able to pocket over sixty pounds. What a prize for a hard-up and worried expectant father! What a handful to go home with!

How thoroughly we trimmed that wheat as it came pouring into our hold from the corn bins in the Millwall Dock! Jerry, the mate, knew how I was situated and put his back into the job as never before. Sweating and covered with dust we shovelled the wheat into the 'wings' and 'cupboards' to make sure that the ship could take all the cargo allotted to her and also to put her in the best possible trim for a hard winter's passage.

She was deeply laden by the time we got it all in and I remember one or two barge skippers saying that they would not like to go to Yarmouth in January with all that weight in. But every ton meant a sorely-needed pound on the freight, and I would have put some down in the cabin rather than leave any behind for lack of stowage space.

The skies glowered down on us as we sailed out of the dock into the river, and it was obvious to any sailorman that there was going to be a lot of wind in the near future. From north-west a light breeze had backed slowly round to south-west to the accompaniment of a miserable drizzle; and as we headed through the broader reaches below Gallions it was still shifting slowly against the sun and became practically southerly in direction.

We reached Greenhithe at dusk and went ashore for a good stock of rations. There were no other coasting barges lying there, so there was no-one to argue with about the evil portents of the weather. I was glad of that because, blow high or low, the *Martinet* was going to Yarmouth in a hurry and I should not have been very patient with any warnings and head shakings. When I had seen everything put aboard I went off home on the bus, telling the crew to bring the boat to the causeway for me at seven o'clock in the morning.

It was January and there was a lull in the bombing. The weather was against the German airmen and, moreover, the war-lords of that brutal people had begun to realise that the obstinate inhabitants of the British Isles (and London in particular) would not be bullied, bashed and battered into submission. The Hun had called off his skydogs that they might lick the grievous wounds inflicted by the young men who flew the fighter planes of the Royal Air Force. I was therefore thankful that my home was likely to be left in peace while I was away at sea.

Chapter Sixteen

IN THE DARKNESS OF A JANUARY MORNING I rode a bicycle along the lonely road that stretches across Dartford Heath. At the cross roads beyond I had to dismount and undergo the scrutiny of a policeman who guarded the entry into what was known as a defence zone. The spectre of invasion still loomed large in our daily lives in spite of the lull in the bombing.

Before I could enter Dartford I had to prove to the policeman's satisfaction my business there and also establish my identity. Being a registered seaman this was not difficult and the whole interrogation was carried through, in less than a minute, with that cheerful camaraderie which Metropolitan policemen display when they are satisfied that all is well.

The blackness of the night was beginning to ease as I passed through the town and up East Hill into the cement country. That is a stretch of countryside, once one of the most beautiful parts of Kent and overlooking the lower reaches of the river, which has been desecrated by the white dust from the tall chimneys of several huge cement works which are clustered in the district. For nearly ten miles the roof-tops, trees, bushes—everything—are laden with this repulsive coating. I have been told that it could be prevented, but apparently there is no practical law to stop the polluting of great areas of lovely scenery and possibly injuring the health of thousands of men, women and children who daily breathe this awful atmosphere.

Into whitened Greenhithe I rode—one of the worst of all the villages suffering under 'cementism'—and I could see by the smoke from the factories that there was a strong wind blowing from the south-west. Leaving my bicycle in the local butcher's backyard, I went down the slippery causeway and gave the distinctive hail by which the mate knew that I was about.

Soon I could see Jerry's broad figure swaying in the dim light as he sculled the boat ashore.

'Plenty of wind,' he said, by way of greeting.

'It's the right way for us,' I replied, 'and she'll go down along the sand by to-night; perhaps the "sheers" or south-west middle.'

'Good,' said the mate, for he never liked to be lying about at anchor and would rather punch a gale of wind and fail than sit and wait for better weather. And he knew that I would not have come away from home if I had not been determined to get under way and make Yarmouth in the quickest possible time.

I found that Jerry had got everything ready on board—mainsail loosed, jib unfurled and anchor chain hove short. In a matter of ten minutes the *Martinet* was drawing out of the bight and we could see the dark outline of the ships and craft lying off Swanscombe.

We gybed and set the topsail. The cook came up with mugs of cocoa. In good heart we started to reduce the hundred and ten miles of salt water which we had to traverse to arrive off Yarmouth pier-heads.

With a spring ebb under her the old ship hustled down through Gravesend Reach, the Lower Hope and Sea Reach like a racehorse. Off Southend we swept through the great crowd of ships mustering for the morning convoys. The sight of our little cloud of canvas brought many a cheery wave and shout of greeting from their decks.

I prayed that no Naval Control launch would dart out and try and bring us to a standstill with some ridiculous orders. We saw several Control vessels, but they were busy with the big ships and we sped on, unhindered, through the boom gate and out into the freedom of the West Swin.

There was no sign of German aircraft, although we could hear faintly the rumble of gunfire somewhere to the south-east—probably an attack on a convoy in the region of the Downs or Dover Straits.

The flood tide had started by the time we were down past the wreck of the *Rosme,* a barge which had been blown up by one of the new acoustic mines. The mine had gone off astern of her but the after end of the barge was blown in. The mate was paralysed down in the cabin but the skipper hauled him out of the sinking vessel and held him up for something like three hours before they were rescued. He was decorated by the King for his courage and presence of mind.

It was no easy job navigating the narrow tidal channels of the Thames Estuary, especially on the ebb, because many of the buoys and marks had been removed, and even misplaced, to deceive the enemy should he attempt to land on our shores. There wasn't much to stop him in those days except the Royal Navy, R.A.F. and the civilian population. The Army was still being rebuilt and re-equipped after the disasters on the Continent. They were still a 'scratch side', as the soldiers themselves used to say.

In the evening we sounded our way into an anchorage known to Essexmen as 'Abraham's bosom'. It is a desolate spot, many miles offshore, where the Maplin Sands are divided from the Whitaker Shoals by a semi-circle of water from three to four fathoms in depth at low tide. These shoals form a breakwater except at high water and the bottom provides excellent holding ground. I have lain there more times than I can remember in all sorts of weather except when the wind has been easterly. From that direction the anchorage is exposed and dangerous.

We rolled about and had to pump until the flood tide was done, but as the water drained off the sand the barge lay still and the pump handle could safely be put to bed for the night.

The long night done, we were under way again, but the wind was lighter and had edged further to the southward again. There was little doubt that some uncommonly rough weather was in the offing and the seamanlike thing to do would have been to run across the Spitway in the late afternoon and up into the safety of the River Colne. In fact, the Naval instructions said that barges were supposed to go into Colne before proceeding as far as Harwich; but no one ever took any notice of that. In any case, the idea of being windbound in Colne did not appeal to us at all. I wanted to get to Yarmouth as rapidly as possible. So I kept the Naval routeing documents out of sight, so as not to discourage myself, and sailed down round the North-East Gunfleet, skirting the wrecks of the big ships mined near the West Rocks, and across to the Rough buoy.

Abreast of Harwich we could just discern the Examination Vessel (to whom we were supposed to report) in the distance but we turned our attention to immediate tasks and did not notice her make any signal.

We could have run round Orfordness and past Aldeburgh by sunset but the weather looked so threatening that I decided to bring up under the lee of the Whiting Sand. There is good anchoring ground there and, although much too exposed to be comfortable, it would be better than a night in the open North

Sea. Also we were in a position to go back to Harwich harbour or round the Ness or make for Yarmouth Roads according to what sort of 'spoon drifter' the gods had in store for us.

A third consideration was that we were outside the zone of Naval Control vessels and were therefore free to do as we liked (more or less) except during the hours of darkness when we might be sunk by gunfire if discovered under way near the coast. It was always a great relief to sailing barge skippers to feel that they were beyond the clutches of the Naval Control launches and Examination boats.

The afternoon was grey and foreboding and we could not see the setting sun. Just before darkness fell the wind, which had fallen away to a few puffs from the southward, began to freshen and kick up a bit of a popple. There was already a fair swell rolling northward and I did not like the prospect of a wind that would whip those tops into white caps.

Except for an occasional cat-nap, I did not attempt to sleep that night. I knew that if the sea got up dangerously we might be unable to get our anchor and reach the safety of either the open sea or Harwich harbour. And the *Martinet,* in spite of some repairs having been done by a young shipwright, still made a lot of water unless she was able to lie quietly.

The night seemed endless. The mate and I pumped and watched and watched and pumped until an hour before dawn. We let Freddie sleep one of his unconscious sleeps in the forecastle so that we should have at least one fresh man for the next day.

It took us nearly an hour to heave our anchor up, and with the mainsail and jib we 'toed and heeled' round the Ness into the white water of the tide-rip off the lighthouse. We had to set the topsail off Aldeburgh to hold the spars steadier. The sea there was more abeam and we rolled our weather rail under at times. I was thankful that Jerry was a strong and agile fellow. He had to be to go up and loose the topsail, for the main rigging had stretched a bit and, as it tightened and slacked each side with the rolling of the ship, the ratlines threatened to jerk the mate out of the hounds. Once his feet flew from under him, but he had a good grip on the tail of the clewline block and crashed back into the rigging as she rolled the other way.

With the topsail set the barge careered along like a mad horse. Freddie cooked the dinner and then came aft as my lee helmsman. The mate went below for a rest and a meal. I had to make him do it, as he would never spare himself when there was work to be done and I had constantly to remind him not to tire himself out in case anything untoward happened later on.

It was blowing hard from about south-south-east (a wicked quarter), but Freddie and I managed to steer her fairly straight. He was a wiry, muscular individual, and when the *Martinet* occasionally took a wild root to windward on the crest of a wave he pushed and pulled manfully to help me straighten her up again.

There was a loud belch from below and I knew that the mate had finished his dinner. I sent Freddie down to eat, Jerry taking his place at the wheel. While the third hand was below I made clear to Jerry the plan of action I had in mind.

I wanted to save our ebb down to Yarmouth Roads so that the tide would still be running out of the harbour or else slack when we arrived off the pier-heads. There would be no sense in signalling for a tug because towing would be more dangerous than sailing with such a heavy sea running. We would, therefore, have to enter the harbour under sail. I felt sure I could get her in there with the wind to the east of south provided the flood tide had not started. To do so then would only be to court a catastrophe. If we did not get there before the flood came then the wind would have eased or veered off the land and we could run past Yarmouth if necessary and round the Cockle to find an anchorage of some sort, or might even bring up in the Roads.

By explaining to the mate what was in my mind I knew that he would know what to do when the time came with hardly any orders from me.

When the third hand had had his fill he returned to the wheel and Jerry took charge while I ate. He was a good helmsman and quite trustworthy in any sort of weather. He had come along wonderfully during the last few months and had now spent a year in the *Martinet*. From his amateur yachting habits he had got into the way of a professional seaman and I could see that it would not take many years to mould him into a bargemaster. He was a lover of all ships of sail and he had the strength, agility and intelligence to tackle any task with which a seafarer might be faced. All he needed was experience—and that is the most necessary and long drawn-out process of all in becoming a genuine sailorman.

Having wrestled with a meal below on the lee locker (it was hopeless to try and eat off the table) I felt that we were all ready for anything. As old George Mead used to say, 'I'm a poor tool on an empty guts', and there was a lot of wisdom in the old skipper's words. Well fed, a man can accomplish much that he has not the heart to do if his bodily energies have flagged and need re-fuelling.

I was beginning to feel quite satisfied and confident as we overtook and passed a couple of steam trawlers wallowing and bucking in the Stanford Channel. From the bridge of one of them someone waved a cap to us as a sort of friendly gesture.

We closed the land and entered Lowestoft North Road, when a great dark cloud swept down on us from seaward. White specks began driving across the deck. It was snow, and a fierce blizzard was upon us almost without warning.

For a moment I thought we should have to let our topsail blow out, but when the head was let run down it fell clear of everything and nestled quietly under the lee of the mainsail. Jerry then clewed the sheet in, went aloft and secured it with a gasket. By the time he reached the deck again the snow was so thick that we could not see the land and the wind was screaming through the rigging as though all hell had been let loose.

The tide was still ebbing strongly. We had only three miles to go. I could not see a ship's length ahead and had to post Jerry forward as a look-out for other ships and buoys which we might run into. I prayed that the snow would lift so that we could see the harbour entrance. There was a lot of water surging to and fro on the midship decks and I wondered if the recent repairs were keeping the water out (which I doubted) as I could not spare anyone for the pumps.

I sent Freddie forward to tell Jerry to set tight the main topping lift and ease the mainsail a third of the way down. There was no time to take in a proper reef, but I wanted the vessel eased a little to make her better to steer over the bar and through the dangerous whirlpools that form between the two piers.

By great good fortune the snow lightened a little just as we approached the harbour, so that I just caught a glimpse of Gorleston Pier, the southernmost one. I could see the seas battering the stonework and flinging clouds of spray across the watch-tower on the end. My God! Suppose we missed the entrance and hit the pier. That would be the end of things for sure, I thought. But for all the fearsome wind and sea and the blinding snow I knew, now that I had a good bearing of the entrance out of the corner of my eye, that the *Martinet* was going in.

Just as the piers loomed up the port examination vessel, a converted trawler, came pitching up on our weather quarter, some sort of lieutenant bawling a string of routine questions through a microphone about 'Where are you from? Where are you bound? [As though he couldn't see.] What cargo? How many on board? Any foreigners? Have you anything to report? When did you leave London? etc., etc.'

We told him to get out of the way in a manner for which bargemen are well known. He did so and went astern.

On the bar the *Martinet* sheered sharply on the curve of the ebb stream, gybed and hung fire for a moment in a swirl of white water. Then she surged forward until she was inside the extremity of the north pier and, with Jerry to help me at the wheel, we drove her in with another vicious squall breaking upon us.

A crowd of soldiers gathered and watched our little struggle. I saw the red signal lights flashing to stop all outgoing traffic and thus give us all the room possible to get the barge round Brush Bend and into safety.

We gybed again at the bend, steadied her, and up the Haven we went like a train. Jerry heaved a sigh. 'Bloody good,' he said, as we got into the smooth water.

'Thank the Lord we're in!' I replied.

We went up the long harbour so fast that we had a job to stop her even with the ebb tide against us. Long before we reached the place where we generally tied up we stowed all sail, but the wind was so strong that it looked as though we might have to let go our anchor and a lot of chain to stop her hitting the bridge at the end.

Luckily for us there happened to be an old barge skipper standing on the Haven bridge, George Quinton, who used to sail the *Britisher*. Seeing in an instant that we required someone to check us with a long stem rope he ran down the quay at top speed and gave us a shout.

I ran her close to the quay and Jerry hove the rope ashore at the first attempt. Quinton caught it and checked us first on one mooring ring and then on another until he had traversed about three hundred yards of the quay. The worthy George then brought us to a halt, thereby saving us a deal of anchor drill.

The next day we were towed up the Yare to Norwich. The cargo was not quite dry, but the merchants did not complain. At some mills the stevedores will take five shillings off the skipper to mix the wet wheat in with the dry because it saves them the labour of having to put it in bags. But of course they don't do anything like that at Norwich.

By the time we were empty and being towed down to
Yarmouth the weather had become beautifully fine with a
moderate breeze blowing from the north. We put to sea in the
morning and had a 'yacht cruise' passage home, arriving off
Greenhithe exactly a week after we had left there. I was richer by
£60 and Jerry by £30.

The day after we got back I heard in the White Hart that in the
same blizzard that had caught us off Yarmouth poor old Frank
Day had lost the *Martha*. She had been driven ashore on the Naze
and become a total wreck. The skipper and his two sons had been
rescued, with difficulty, by the Walton lifeboat. He could have
run her into Harwich but was not able to reach the harbour
approaches before nightfall, and the Naval Control Regulations
laid down emphatically that no barge must approach the harbour
during darkness. No alternative was given for sailing vessels
under stress of weather. So Frank let go his anchor just below
Walton Pier in the vain hope that the barge would hold there until
daylight. Before the night was very old the anchor chain parted
and the gallant old *Martha* crashed to her doom on the rocky
headland. The previous day he had lost his second anchor, but ten
anchors would not have saved her in such weather or on such
treacherous holding ground.

Another of our company's barges, the racing champion
Cambria, lost her mainsail while in the Wallet and had her
topsail split from head to sheet but managed to weather the Naze
and get into Harwich before nightfall. The examination boat had
tried to hold her up off the entrance, but the *Cambria* kicked up
her heels and left the Navy boat behind. The latter could not
catch the barge until she had passed right through Harwich
harbour and reached the anchorage in the mouth of the River
Orwell. The skipper of the barge then had to apologise to the
lieutenant for disregarding the latter's hail.

'I'm sorry, sir,' old Cully, the skipper, said with his tongue in
his cheek, 'but we couldn't stop.'

Chapter Seventeen

THE WORTHY FREDDIE DISAPPEARED in Ipswich while we were discharging linseed at the Oil Mill by Stoke Bridge. I had to sign him off the ship's articles in his absence, filling in the required details on his behalf and inserting under the heading 'Cause of Leaving' the incriminating word 'Deserted'.

He had gone ashore in the morning and I have never seen him from that day to this. Although the mate and I made enquiries from the police and the local hospital as to his fate, we could not trace him.

Perhaps he joined another ship or went back to his beloved fair-grounds, there once more to relieve the unsuspecting joy-riders of their proper change. Perhaps it was his body that was hauled out of Ipswich Dock some days later and laid in the mortuary with the label of 'unidentified seaman'. I was not there to see, and although one or two Ipswich bargemen said that the corpse looked like him they would not swear to it.

Having duly entered him as a deserter and reported the matter in the proper quarters, my official dealings with him ended. He was one of those wandering, homeless souls, to all intents and purposes cut off from all parental and family connections, befriending none and by none befriended. There are thousands like him and one often finds them at sea. If they live, no-one cares. If they die, no-one cares about that either. So it was with Freddie.

My immediate concern was to get the ship back to London. There being no third hand to be found, it did not take the mate and me many moments to decide to sail her home two-handed. It was only a matter of sixty miles or so and no open-sea work to do.

Our decision was probably hastened by a fair wind from east-north-east. Away we went, sweating the canvas on her as the little local motor-boat towed her down the 'Cut' and out into the Orwell River. We sailed sedately down the narrow channel, through Harwich harbour, and then squared off up the Wallet with a smart breeze dead aft.

The night after leaving Ipswich we anchored near the Ridge

buoy in the entrance to the River Crouch. It was a safe, snug
berth and we intended to be off up-swin to London in the early
morning.

The sails having been stowed and everything made shipshape
on deck, Jerry and I retired below with a pair of nicely edged
appetites for our usual evening meal—a sort of high tea taken
rather late but not quite late enough to be called supper. We made
a practice of it for years and it suited us during war-time when
the regulations compelled us to anchor during the hours of
darkness. If the weather was at all reasonable we could say that
the day's work was done and sit down in peace and comfort.

Just before we ranged alongside the cabin table we heard the
noise of a motor-boat and went on deck again in answer to a
rather faint-hearted hail. It was a small patrol boat, obviously
manned by amateurs but lately recruited to the sea or possibly by
inexperienced yachtsmen. Her skipper wanted to know the usual
details ('where from, where bound,' etc.) and I told him. He then
chootled off up-river towards Shore-ends.

Thinking we had seen the last of him and having no other
cares, we fell-to upon fried sausages, onions and mash, swilled
down with great mugs of tea and followed by a pipe of tobacco
and a musical programme on the wireless.

We had shut the cabin door, and the fire, drawn up by the
easterly wind, glowed cheerfully.

We were enjoying these simple luxuries without the slightest
notion of what was going on outside until the mate said he
thought he heard that motor-boat again. We turned off the
wireless and sure enough we could hear the propeller churning
the water near us. Noises in the water are very distinct when
below decks. I went up the stairs to investigate.

At the doorway of the deckhouse which led to the companion
I met with a horrible shock. I found myself staring at the end of a
machine-gun, pointed threateningly at me from the deck of the
motor-boat by a dim figure who seemed to be in an awful temper.
He was saying, 'I'll show them. I'll show them. I'll make them
answer.'

My life was saved by someone in the stern of the boat
shouting in a voice full of alarm:

'Don't shoot, skipper. Don't shoot. There's someone standing there.'

That was me.

'Why didn't you answer my hail?' demanded the skipper haughtily.

'I didn't hear you,' I said. 'You should learn to shout.' I knew that most of those ex-office lads were not well versed in seamen's ways. When a seaman wants to hail someone or get aboard his ship he learns, through experience, that he can cool his heels for many a long hour unless he kicks up an unholy hullaballoo. This he does, whistling, shouting, and making far reaching noises, interspersed with the name of the ship required, so that he can be heard for miles around and often in the next county.

But these newcomers to sea-life used to cruise round muttering 'I say' and expecting us to take notice of them. I had been approached by such faint mumblings before and I immediately suspected that these people in the patrol boat had failed to make full use of their lungs.

However, the skipper was furious. He had felt insulted at not being answered promptly, had threatened to fire on the *Martinet* in a fit of temper, and was not in the least calmed by my eventual reply. I saw no reason for all this, seeing that we had previously given him our details, and told him so. I felt not a little nettled that I might have had my body riddled with bullets by this idiot had not the other fellow seen me and spoken up in time.

That danger having now passed I took every opportunity to pour scorn and sarcasm upon the officer in charge as a sort of revenge for his high-handedness. He demanded to know what cargo we were carrying. We had none, being light and high up out of the water. Any seaman with half an eye could have seen that the *Martinet* was empty.

'Did you ever see a loaded barge standing up out of the water like a church?' I jibed. 'Can't you see we're only drawing three feet forward? Shine your torch there and have a look. Why can't you use a bit of common sense, you blank so-and-so?'

All this drove the patrol skipper nearly crazy. .

'I'm sending an armed party aboard. Lower a ladder at once,' he shouted angrily.

'What do you think we are?' I answered. 'The *Queen Mary*? We haven't got a ladder and if we had I wouldn't lower it. If

anyone wants to board this barge they can damn well climb up
the side the same as we have to.'

I suggested that he bring his motor-boat alongside, for there
was a strong spring ebb running. But it looked as though he did
not know how to set about doing that, for he ordered two hands
away in a tiny dinghy only about ten feet long.

First they had a dreadful frap-up through one man unhooking
the forward davit tackle while the after one was still fast. As the
motor-boat was going slow ahead all the time to stem the tide,
the bow of the dinghy swung round and its occupants were being
towed stern first in an exceedingly dangerous fashion. The
painter had not been made fast and the stern was hanging half out
of the water, suspended by the after tackle.

Jerry and I sat on the hatches and passed remarks and offered
hints which were not appreciated. Neither were all these remarks
in the best of taste. But it was the only way we could get our own
back on this imperious officer.

When at last the two men in the dinghy got it adrift they were
carried downstream from the *Martinet,* and it did not seem to
occur to their superior to tow them up slightly ahead of the barge
so that they could sheer over to us with the tide. They set to and
rowed vigorously with two rather small paddles, hindered
somewhat by the fact that they wore heavy coats and were
cluttered up with rifles and ammunition to enforce their authority
when they reached the *Martinet.*

They rowed and they rowed and they rowed. As the tide
swept them astern of us they quickened their strokes to an almost
frantic pace. Both men were on the big side and they presented,
to us, a very funny spectacle in so small a dinghy.

The officer aboard the motor boat did nothing to help them.
He just strutted up and down his miniature deck, obviously
fuming and perhaps wondering why his men took so long to row
over to us.

At last the armed party, on the point of exhaustion, got to
within about fifteen yards of us and, out of sheer sympathy for
their plight, we floated a heaving line down to them and hauled
their cockleshell alongside.

They had no idea how to get aboard an empty, high-sided
barge, and in any case their arms and backs must have ached too

much to heave their heavy bodies up. Rather hastily, they both gripped the covering board (the edge of the deck) and clung there, hanging on by their finger tips. The dinghy drifted from under them and for a moment I thought they were going to lose their grip and drown.

Jerry and I leaned over the rail and grasped them by the shoulders but could not pull them up until we had relieved them of their rifles, which we threw on to the hatches. We then hove the men up, hand over hand, by the back of their coats, coming eventually to the seats of their trousers, by which we finally toppled them over the rail like two bags of barley.

They then picked themselves up and we handed them back the rifles.

Trying to assume some air of dignity, one of them said: 'We demand to see your papers.'

We led them down below and they seemed glad to sit in front of the fire. The mate, a kind-hearted soul, took pity on their condition and gave them each a cup of tea.

I thought that a fitting end to this comedy, which might easily have been a tragedy, would be to deny them that which they sought to inquire into. I felt sure that they did not know a ship's papers from a mission hymn-sheet. So while they drank their tea I rummaged in my drawer and pulled out the ship's assignment (a document concerning the plan and construction of the vessel), an out of date transire and an old Bill of Lading, all of which happened to be tied together with a piece of silk which made them look like valuable papers.

These I handed to the leader of the two-man armed party. He unfolded the assignment, glanced at it with a show of authority, off-handedly turned over the old transire and Bill of Lading and seemed satisfied. He handed them back to me, not knowing that the ship's papers (her register, licence, customs clearance, Admiralty orders and route instructions) lay in the locker behind him.

'Your papers seem quite in order, captain,' he remarked briefly. 'I'm sorry we have had to trouble you, but when you did not answer our hail the skipper became suspicious. Routine, y'know, what!'

And off they went, leaving Jerry and me to our peaceful cabin comforts and to reflect on what silly asses the war had brought upon the water.

• • • • •

Apart from the new dangers of war the *Martinet* was not content to leave me alone for very long. She must needs have another try at knocking my brains out during the winter days.

It was on a trip to Yarmouth. We had a bit of a tussle to get down into the roads. The wind had edged from north-west to north-east (dead ahead) as we slashed along between Southwold and Lowestoft at a smart pace.

I was getting rather doubtful about making Yarmouth at all, and mournfully considered the prospect of being forced to turn her round and run back to Hollesley Bay or, perhaps, even Harwich. It is bitter indeed to be denied the fruits of one's labours when within sight of the port of destination. So we kept plugging away to windward, determined not to give up with only seven miles left out of the hundred and ten we had to sail.

The north-east breeze freshened and we could see heavy seas breaking along the low, sandy shore. But it was not so bad that we could not get ahead and that night we let go our anchor, and a great scope of chain, in Lowestoft North road.

It was a bad night and much of it was spent on the pumps or at anchor watch. I did not like the look of things in the least but put my hope in the prospect of a better dawn.

I might as well have put my hopes in the Devil, for the first light of day told me that we were in for trouble. The spring flood was running hard to the southward and our anchor-chain was bar-taut most of the time. The seas were not really dangerous, but too rough to give us much hope of being able to heave that anchor up. In any case, the wind and tide were against us and if we were able to get under way we could only run back to Harwich. It was obvious that we must get our anchor on the first of the weather-going ebb. Then the wind would blow the ship up against the tide to her anchor and there would be but little strain on the cable.

At the appropriate time we turned to, got the anchor, and set a scrap of sail so that we could get her down off Yarmouth, wearing her round each tack instead of trying to bring her up into the wind. She would never have come about each time unless we had set a lot of canvas and I had no wish to blow sails away at such a time. Off Yarmouth we jilled her to and fro, waiting for the tug. But no tug came out. Hours and hours went by, but our signals were either unnoticed or unheeded and I grew very worried. I did not want another night in the open in this weather.

Darkness crept over the land and then I knew that the tug would not come. Perhaps she had broken down or for some reason was out of commission. Anyway, we had an unpleasant twelve or fourteen hours to look forward to, and I decided to trust to the anchors.

The mate let go the bower with thirty-five fathoms of chain. She dragged this slowly to the southward while we prepared the second anchor and let it go. Then we gave her fifty fathoms on the first and forty on the second and she brought herself up off Gorleston cliffs.

She held there steadily all night and in the morning we hove the second one up. As the ebb came away we laboured to get the main anchor, for I knew that if the tug did not come this day we must run for shelter.

All went well until the last ten fathoms were left to be hove aboard. The *Martinet* reared her lovely head and the windlass gave a mighty kick. Back flew the handles of that wretched new-fangled contraption and I received a violent blow between the eyes.

I found myself on the deck, strange noises singing in my ears, and blood running into my eyes. The mate and third hand lifted me up. I heard the mate say:

'She nearly had you that time.'

They, too, had been knocked over but were unhurt except for bruises. Not quite certain whether I was in this world or the next, I went back to the windlass and we finished getting the anchor up. She was dragging fast with so little chain out and was edging towards the shore.

I then discovered that I was not so badly knocked about as I felt and remembered that my hand had been between the iron handle and my head when they came into collision. Otherwise I might have been put out for good.

We had to run her into Lowestoft harbour that afternoon. For three days we lay there while a north-east gale lashed the coast. When it subsided we crept out into the road again and sailed along to Yarmouth.

Those last few miles had taken a lot of effort, not to mention one more attempt on my life by the old devil-ship.

Chapter Eighteen

THE MARTINET WAS NOT TO LIE IDLE for many days at a time. She was soon roped in to help carry the numerous cargoes of cement required in eastern England to build air-raid shelters, gun emplacements, fortifications, airfields, camps and various military establishments. Cement was a priority cargo then, and we were chartered to take as much as we could load to a merchant in Norwich.

Had she been a good tight ship we could have loaded 210 tons, but in view of the fact that she required somewhat extensive repairs I only put 200 tons into her. In spite of a lot of bodging the persistent leaking had never been cured. She needed to have her entire covering board (that is, where the topsides meet the edge of the deck) taken up and renewed. If that had been done she would have been a fine stout ship with many, many years of useful life in front of her.

In fairness, it must be said that the urgent requirements of power vessels in the company's fleet—many of which had been damaged by mines and air attack—came before the needs of an old-fashioned sailing ship.

We loaded our 200 tons at Swanscombe, starting in the evening and working throughout the night, so that we could get clear of the berth by daylight. There was a big steamship coming down-river to start loading about eight in the morning.

There is no time lost at these cement jetties. Work goes on continually, day and night, Sundays, holidays, and sometimes even Christmas Day. These great concerns always seem to me like vast robot colonies where the cement trundles out, the ships, barges and lorries come and go, and the souls of men are smothered (like the countryside) in the choking white dust of the industry.

Having got the *Martinet* off to her anchor in the morning I hastened ashore to Gravesend, where I had to clear out of Customs and get my secret documents from the Admiralty office. The mate and third hand were left to batten down the hatches, scrub round and get the barge ready for sea.

On my way back I burdened myself with a huge kit bag of

food. All that remained to be done was to sail to Norwich. By midday we were away down St. Clement's Reach under all four lowers and main topsail and with the boat lashed in the davits. When a bargeman lashes his boat you can bet he's off to sea on that tide and not expecting to bring up in the river any more. The wind was west and that is not a wind to waste when bound to the north-east.

When it was dark we anchored on the edge of the Blythe Sands, had a row with a young patrol officer, allowed him to tow us a few yards to conform with some anchorage regulation, anchored again, called him names, and then completed a half-cold supper.

We had a new third hand with us this time, a young barge-mate out of the river craft who was waiting to take a berth in a motor ship. He was a good seaman and did his job without having to be told what to do. That is a great thing about men in sail who are any good—they don't need telling when there is a job which obviously wants doing. They just go and do it. Men from big steamships or out of the Navy who have tried their luck in the barges can never get used to this idea of working without regular orders. Their sort of discipline simply doesn't work.

I have known sailing barges wherein the skipper and mate have reduced all forms of vocal communication to an absolute minimum. They would go through the whole process of getting under way from a crowded anchorage or carry out a tricky manoeuvre with nothing more than an occasional sign, a nod, or something akin to a grunt. Work on the deck of a barge is quite hard enough without doing a lot of shouting. The skipper of the *Kismet* used to be known as Silent Tom, and the mate told me that he had to watch his eyebrows for any semblance of orders. If the mate anticipated that the topsail would be required he used to get it all ready and then if Tom raised his eyebrows it had to be set. Old Knocker in the *Marguerite* used to have a deaf mate. When getting the barge under way the mate would set such canvas as he thought was necessary and in the proper rotation and Knocker would keep an eye on him and shift his helm accordingly. They never spoke to each other on deck unless there was something really urgent to say. If they went ashore for beer and were seen to exchange a few monosyllables in the boat on the way back you knew that they had had a great number of pints.

We sailed out of Sea Reach at the crack of dawn and made a splendid run down-swin and over the Spitway, coming abreast of the Naze in the late afternoon. By this time our lovely west wind had all but disappeared and in its place came a doubtful breeze from further south. There were threatening clouds driving over us and the mate and I discussed the advisability of going into Harwich for the night.

The *Redoubtable,* a big Mistley-owned barge—one of the finest wooden sailing vessels on the coast—went scooting over the Stone Banks under our lee and I had a good mind to follow her. But the tides were such that we should not be able to get out of harbour in the early morning and therefore should fail to make Yarmouth before the next night.

After we had weighed up all the possibilities I let the *Martinet* run on down to Hollesley Bay and anchored under the highest part of the Whiting Sand. That was about five o'clock. I did not like the way the wind was freshening, but it was just one of those chances forced upon us by the war-time anchor-at-night regulation. We could have been in Yarmouth by midnight under pre-war conditions.

I was somewhat alarmed when we came to pump her out before going below for our evening meal. There was a lot of water in her, much more than I had expected. But we sucked her out and then fell-to round the cabin table. While we thus gorged upon the mighty mound of hash the cook had prepared the mate, who sat next to the bulkhead dividing the cabin from the hold, said that he thought he could hear a lot of water slopping about. We removed a piece of the bulkhead under the mate's bunk and looked into the well. The water was almost on the floor of the hold—and we had sucked the pumps only ten minutes before!

We left the repast half-eaten and hurried up on deck. Both the big pumps aft were got working and the three of us settled down to regular spells, two pumping while one rested. After half an hour of this I went below to see how much was left in her. To my horror there was no difference—if anything, she had more water in her than when we had abandoned our meal and re-started pumping.

It was pitch dark now and there was not much hope of finding where the leak was, especially as the barge was deeply-laden. I had a look round with a torch, but apart from an old leak in the counter (on which a shipwright had spent an entire day recently without making the slightest improvement) I could not find any place bad enough to warrant all this pumping.

There was only one thing left to do—pump all night and get her into some sort of harbour—anywhere—as soon as it was light. In these ominous times all the beaches were mined as a defence against the probable invader and it was not possible to save a vessel in distress by beaching her. She would only be blown to bits if not first sunk by a salvo from the shore batteries. And all the harbours were bolted and barred at night by defence booms and nets. So there was nothing to be done except try and keep her afloat with the pumps until daylight allowed us to make a move.

Eleven o'clock. The pumps were just about holding their own. Then the starboard one choked. Frantically we took it to pieces and lay flat on the deck, the seas breaking over us and washing through our clothes, to reach down the pipe in a desperate attempt to clear it. Each of us had a try in turn but the stoppage was down in the very bowels of the ship. In the end we had to resort to a small pump on the after deck, but this one threw only about a third as much water as the other type.

From then on the water in the hold gained slowly but surely on the pumps, but we could have kept her safely afloat until the morning had not a strong wind got up about midnight, causing a short, steep sea to come breaking across the Whiting Sand. The *Martinet* began to labour heavily. I did not like her ugly, sluggish lurch as the water sloshed from one side of her to the other.

During my spells off the pumps I took careful soundings with the hand lead and made sure that she was not dragging her anchor. She rode to thirty-five fathoms and the anchor's hold was never broken.

In our desperate plight I was reminded of the old tale of the *Martinet* being a killer. She had tried all manner of means to do me injury or bring a bloody end to my life; and it seemed that, all other things having failed, she was going to try and drown me and all my crew. She might half fill herself so that we abandoned ship and then miraculously survive while we perished in the lifeboat in an attempt to get ashore. What a triumph that would be for her!

Things went badly for us about two o'clock in the morning.

The wind and sea increased and the ship leaked all the faster as a result. Lower and lower in the water she settled and, although still riding well to her cable, her motions became those of a stricken vessel. I went below and found that the water was nearly two feet deep on the cabin floor, which was higher than the level of the floor in the hold. Mats, papers and odds and ends were washing miserably to and fro. The drawer in which I kept my clothes was full of dirty bilge water. Locker doors had jammed with the straining of the ship and I had to force them open with a crowbar.

Slipping and sliding in the muck that had been washed aft from the bilges I got hold of the water-tight tins that contained distress rockets and flares. These I passed up to the third hand while Jerry kept the big pump going in the hope of our being able to stick to the ship until daybreak. I was becoming doubtful. In fact it was not very pleasant blundering about below decks up to my knees in water and knowing that, being cement loaded, the ship might take a sudden plunge to her doom.

Each in turn went below and put his personal belongings into kit bags, finally bringing up a stock of hard biscuits, condensed milk, corned beef and the usual items that shipwrecked mariners endeavour to have beside them. It was no good taking any chances. She might not last until morning.

She sank so low in the water that eventually the tops of the pumps were submerged. It was half-past two. We were wet through and the wind seemed very cold. We could feel sleet driving above the spray. Pumping was no longer of any use—or even possible.

A gloomy trio, we mustered aft under the lee of the wheelhouse. Our prospects were dark indeed. If we took to the lifeboat and lived through the breakers in the bay we were faced with the risk of landing on a steep shingle bank down which the pebbles and stones rushed at amazing speed with each recoiling wave. It was a bad place to try and beach a small boat. And even if we succeeded in getting ashore we should almost certainly be either shot by the soldiers on guard or blown to smithereens by a land-mine.

For two hours we hung on to the side of the wheelhouse, cold, tired and hungry, wondering how long she would last. One more inspection below brought me to a decision. There was so much water in her that she might sink at any moment, though she might wallow in a half-sunken state for many hours, as wooden vessels often do.

We lit a rocket but it misfired, hit the mizzenmast and went straight down into the sea. We tried another and were more successful. It soared skywards in a graceful arc, leaving a trail of sparks behind it. Immediately afterwards we lit a flare so that if anyone on shore had seen our rocket, they could then determine the position of our vessel by bearings. It was half-past four. I hoped that the coastguards at Orfordness would see our signals. At least we were advertising the fact that we were in trouble. I felt bound to do that as the lives of the crew depended on my discretion. Whatever risks I like to take myself, I was in no way entitled to gamble with other people's lives.

Our supply of signals was limited, so we waited twenty minutes before we again sent up a rocket and a flare. This we continued to do until about eight o'clock, when the dim streaks of dawn could be seen over the North Sea.

The *Martinet* was practically awash. Only her proud head and shapely counter were above sea level. I estimated, although I could not be certain, that since she had not already gone down she would last several hours more.

It was the third hand who first saw that our salvation was at hand. His keen young eyes spotted something bobbing up and down in the white-capped seas to the eastward. It was the Aldeburgh lifeboat coming to our assistance.

Now that help was near I felt a grim reluctance to leave the ship. I imagined that the old devil in her was laughing at me. Apart from that, the *Martinet* had been my home for practically two years, and I had grown fond of the old vessel in spite of her bad reputation. And although I had decided that the time had come to abandon her, there lingered within me a dim spark of hope that perhaps she might be saved. Common sense told me that her days were about to end, but I could not bring myself to realise it. But there was no holding back now. The lifeboatmen were shouting to us to get ready to jump as they manoeuvred to bring their craft alongside.

It was not an easy matter for the coxwain to take us off the *Martinet,* half-submerged as she was, rolling heavily and with the seas breaking right over her. He brought his boat round in a wide sweep under our port quarter, but at that moment the barge took a wild sheer away from him and the gulf between us was too far to jump.

We hung on while the lifeboat motored down to leeward again and at the second attempt she rose on a sea and almost landed on our deck. As she crashed into our bulwarks Jerry and the third hand slung their kitbags into her and jumped. As she descended into the hollow of the sea I followed them and we all landed in a heap in her cockpit.

The coxwain had come alongside on the tideward side of the barge to make sure of getting us off and he had some difficulty in getting away from the stricken vessel. With three sickening jolts the lifeboat struck the *Martinet* and the seas descended mercilessly on both the rescuers and the rescued. At last the little boat's head was pushed clear and she plunged out to windward.

'Which of you be the captain?' shouted the burly, red-faced coxswain, shrouded in dripping yellow oilskins.

When he had identified me we had a brief conference on the
fate of the *Martinet*.

'You 'adn't reckoned on tryin' to save 'er?' asked the
coxswain with a forlorn hope of profitable salvage.

I looked over at the *Martinet* and shook my head. Her midship
decks were no longer visible above water, even when she rose on
a crest, and she had that unnatural, out-of-time motion which
spells the doom of a vessel in distress.

'She won't last long now,' agreed the coxswain. 'She's too far
gone. We'd better leave 'er and get you chaps ashore. Go t'hell if
you don't look some'ut wet and cold. This 'ere sleet don't 'elp,
neither. Where's that there bottle of rum, Horace? Open 'er up.
Them biscuits, too.'

The opening of the rum bottle was performed with great
alacrity and all the crew had a swig before it came round to us.
Apparently the only chance they ever had of getting a tot was
when they rescued someone, and they were not slow to grasp the
opportunity. Not that I blamed them in the least when I learned of
their gallant efforts to come to our assistance. As we chugged
northwards to Aldeburgh, running before the wind and careering
giddily down the steep-sided seas, the crew told me their story.

The coastguards at Orfordness had seen our rockets and had
telephoned to Aldeburgh. The lifeboat crew were called from
their beds at five o'clock in the morning and they hurried down
to the beach. There was a heavy sea breaking onshore and there
was no hope of getting the biggest lifeboat afloat because an
enemy air attack had damaged the slipway the day before.

The only thing they could do was to try and haul off the little
'summer' boat, as they called her. This boat was designed for
minor rescue operations in fine weather and was hardly fit to be
launched in a winter's gale. But these Suffolk men are a hard lot,
and, although there is no harbour at Aldeburgh to shelter them
from onshore winds, they have never failed to go out in answer to
a call for help.

Waist deep in the icy water, with the blinding sleet driving
almost horizontally, they struggled to get the little cockleshell
afloat. Three times men and boat were flung back on to the
shingle beach but at the fourth attempt they got her off and drove
her out through the breakers.

They deserved that rum.

'Go steady with that bottle, me lads,' laughed the coxswain. 'Don't forget the shipwrecked mariners.'

By the time everyone had had his turn with the bottle it was empty. By a nice piece of judgement there was just enough left in the bottom for the last man, the entire operation taking not more than three or four minutes.

'When we arrived off Aldeburgh beach the coxswain told me that there was a boom defence and minefield between us and the shore. He would not be able to beach his boat as he would in the ordinary way. She would have to be brought broadside to the breakers to get in through the narrow gap and round the inner shoal.

'You'll get a wet shirt when she hits,' he warned us.

He was a middle-aged man and a boatman of great experience, but his weather-beaten old face was grim and anxious as we headed for the shore: We surged through the gap in the boom and slewed round so that the seas came at us right abeam. The boat was thrown violently almost on to her beam ends and there were cries of 'Hold fast, she's going to hit.'

As she struck the beach the seas broke right over our heads and the boat all but capsized. I found myself sprawling in the backwash and some soldiers ran down into the water and dragged me up. Jerry and the third hand were wading ashore, hauling their sodden kitbags after them.

Ten minutes later we were having a hot bath in a water-front hotel. The people on shore had everything ready for us—dry clothes, hot food, hot whisky and cigarettes. They are accustomed to playing host to shipwrecked mariners in Aldeburgh.

After we had eaten I telephoned the Orfordness coastguards and they told me that the *Martinet* was still visible, wallowing half-submerged in a heavy sea. The wind was of gale force and they did not think she would last much longer.

A few hours later she sank. That was the end of the wicked old *Martinet*, last of the 'boomie' barges.

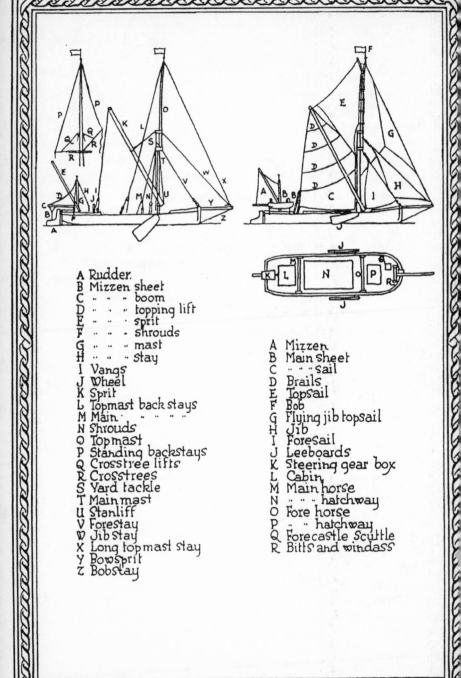

A Rudder.
B Mizzen sheet
C „   „   „ boom
D „   „   „ topping lift
E „   „   „ sprit
F „   „   „ shrouds
G „   „   „ mast
H „   „   „ stay
I Vangs
J Wheel
K Sprit
L Topmast back stays
M Main „   „   „
N Shrouds
O Topmast
P Standing backstays
Q Crosstree lifts
R Crosstrees
S Yard tackle
T Mainmast
U Stanliff
V Forestay
W Jib stay
X Long topmast stay
Y Bowsprit
Z Bobstay

A Mizzen
B Main sheet
C „ „ sail
D Brails
E Topsail
F Bob
G Flying jib topsail
H Jib
I Foresail
J Leeboards
K Steering gear box
L Cabin
M Main horse
N „ „ hatchway
O Fore horse
P „ „ hatchway
Q Forecastle Scuttle
R Bitts and windass